Ainsley's
Good mood food

Ainsley's
Good mood food

easy, comforting meals to lift your spirits

Ainsley Harriott

EBURY
PRESS

1

Ebury Press, an imprint of Ebury Publishing
20 Vauxhall Bridge Road, London SW1V 2SA

Ebury Press is part of the Penguin Random House
group of companies whose addresses can be found
at global.penguinrandomhouse.com

Penguin
Random House
UK

First published by Ebury Press in 2021

www.penguin.co.uk

A CIP catalogue record for this book is available
from the British Library

ISBN 978-152914831-2

TV Series Home Economist: Claire Bassano
Project Editor: Lisa Pendreigh
Designers: Smith & Gilmour
Photographer: Dan Jones
Food Stylist: Bianca Nice
Props Stylist: Max Robinson

Colour origination by Altaimage, London
Printed and bound by Firmengruppe APPL,
aprinta druck, Wemding, Germany

The authorised representative in the EEA is
Penguin Random House Ireland, Morrison Chambers,
32 Nassau Street, Dublin D02 YH68.

Penguin Random House is committed to a sustainable
future for our business, our readers and our planet.
This book is made from Forest Stewardship Council®
certified paper.

Introduction

There's no two ways about it – food can definitely lift your spirits and put you in a good mood. I first realised this as a young boy watching and helping my mum cook for family and friends. She was a wonderful home cook, and I could see the love she put into her food and the way it would bring a smile to people's faces. The kitchen was always a busy place, full of laughter and music. That's when my love of cooking started. Watching all those happy people enjoying my mum's food is probably what inspired me most to become a chef. I, too, wanted to spread some joy through cooking. Of course, this was followed by many years of training and hard work in restaurant kitchens, but that initial drive never went away. Food doesn't have to be fancy; if it's made with love and passion, it will always bring some happiness – even if it's just from the enjoyment of making and sharing a meal.

Although we've been through some difficult times recently, being kept apart for months on end, in some ways it's helped us to slow down and rediscover the joy of cooking. Whether it's cooking for one, cooking for the kids, or rustling up something special for the community, we've all had the time to look again at our favourite recipes. Old-fashioned casseroles, retro school-dinner recipes and hearty pasta bakes have all had a revival – perhaps as we've looked to the past and to the familiar for a bit of comfort and feel-good nostalgia. Food is so evocative, and the taste, smell and texture of a dish can bring back all sorts of memories. Whether it's the smell of fresh bread baking or a casserole cooking on the stove, food can evoke memories of family, comfort and childhood. Whenever I smell the unique aroma of pimento, or allspice, I'm immediately taken back in time and can see my mum stirring a dutchie pot of tasty Caribbean stew. Food to me is also about sharing, and as we returned to a bit of normality over the summer it was fantastic to get back to eating together. Cooking for my kids, even now they're older, still brings me so much joy, and we often get together for a homemade pizza or curry night.

You can't beat sharing great food, good conversation and a drink or two with family and friends. That's one reason why I love barbecuing and summer dining: there's something magical about cooking and eating outside. Obviously good weather helps, but even on a dull day sharing something like my Fiery BBQ Glazed Pork Ribs with a group of mates is a fabulous thing indeed. As I said years ago in my *Barbecue Bible* – finger-lickin' food is deliciously sociable! Of course, a little splash of booze is also a good way to lift the mood and a dash of rum in a marinade never goes amiss. I had the pleasure of cooking on the beach at the Carbis Bay in St Ives for the series and, even though we had some rainy days, the joy of being outside in the sea air was fantastic. The smell of the barbecue brought a crowd of people to the beach, and it was lovely to be cooking up some delicious recipes in my outdoor kitchen. It was something we perhaps valued even more because of the strange year we'd all been through. I've shared some tasty barbecue recipes in the book for you to enjoy, with colourful salsas and side salads to add some zing. If the weather isn't ideal or you don't have the luxury of a garden, you can always use a chargrill pan to bring the taste of the summer barbecue inside.

Good mood food to me is all about fabulous flavour and I've been lucky enough to have travelled to some exciting places over the years to taste many different cuisines and their unique use of herbs and spices. Spice is an important part of my cooking, and although a dish doesn't need to have too much heat, I like it to have plenty of spice. Whether it's the tang of Middle Eastern sumac in my Sumac Lamb Kofta with Coriander Flatbreads or the smoky hit of sweet paprika in Creole Jambalaya, each spice brings a special flavour. Many spices also have nutritional benefits – turmeric is known to fight inflammation and stimulate serotonin, ginger contains Vitamin B6 to help improve energy levels, and cinnamon apparently helps to lower blood sugars and enhance cognitive processing – all of which must be pretty useful for helping us to feel good. Fresh herbs are so important for adding flavour, and a handful of chopped parsley, coriander or mint can really lift a dish to another level. Herbs are really easy to grow, and I like to have pots of them growing in the kitchen and garden, so that I always have a ready supply. Thyme is one of my favourite herbs and it features in many of my recipes – it's an earthy herb with a subtle, sweet peppery flavour that marries well with other herbs and spices from many different cuisines. It's also said to have a calming effect on the body. I don't know if that's true, but it would be nice to think that my comforting

Jackfruit, Butter Bean & Okra Pimento Pot can also help
you to feel calm from the inside. Of course, I do like things a
bit spicy so if chilli is your thing, you'll find plenty of recipes with
a bit of a kick. Chillies are a great mood booster – when eating
them, your body produces endorphins which give you a sense of
happiness. I use a few different types of chilli in this book, from
the mild heat of the Kashmiri chilli to the very hot and fruity
Scotch bonnet, and tiny yet fiery bird's-eye chilli. You can always
adjust the heat to suit your taste – just check the strength of your
fresh chillies and add as much or as little as you like. To temper
the spice, I love using yoghurt in my cooking or serving it as an
accompaniment. Not only does it add creaminess and flavour it's
also really good for you, so it makes you feel great on the inside
too. Speaking of natural mood boosters, adding a handful of seeds
or nuts to a dish will not only add texture, flavour and richness
but also provide a great source of nutrients and antioxidants.
More importantly, they contain an amino acid responsible for
producing mood-boosting serotonin. Another good reason to
add nuts to your food!

I always like to use fresh citrus in my cooking – a good squeeze
of lemon, lime or orange always boosts the flavour and can make
all the difference to the finished dish. An extra burst of vitamin C
can't be a bad thing either. Using fresh produce – whether it's
fruit, veg, meat or fish – is the best way to ensure great flavour
and is, of course, the most nutritious way. It was great to get
out and about across the country to meet some of our best food
producers. They were so passionate about their produce and
rightly so, whether it was foraging for sea herbs with the
wonderful Alysia Vasey, learning about bees and artisan honey
with the guys from Black Mountain Honey or visiting The
Watercress Company in Hampshire, it was great to see the
love and care that goes into creating their products. When
visiting and chatting to William Chase about his apple cider
vinegar, he said, 'I want people to feel more connected to their
food and appreciate that eating isn't just a process, it's a way
of life,' and I couldn't agree more. Supermarkets these days
have such a wide selection of fresh produce, and you can get
just about anything you need – including many of the Caribbean
fruit and vegetables that used to be so difficult to find – but do
try to support your local and independent grocers, fishmongers,
butchers and farm shops too.

Many of these recipes have suggestions for seasonal swaps and the vegetables can be tweaked to suit whatever you have in the fridge, to save on food waste. I eat meat-free at least a couple of times a week and using seasonal vegetables keeps things interesting. My Caraway & Orange Roasted Vegetables work well with either summer veg or with roasted roots in the autumn or winter. Cooking from scratch is always going to be better for you, so keep your dishes vibrant and colourful by using a variety of fresh produce; not only will your food be beautiful and exciting, it will help you feel good from the inside out. A tasty meal can make my heart sing, soothe my soul and recharge my batteries, and although I like to use plenty of fresh produce, the recipes in this book are the foods that make me feel good rather than instructions on what constitutes a healthy diet. I'm more for balance and applying common sense than restricting what I eat, and you'll find plenty of nutritious family meals, healthy salads and light meals alongside the comforting stews and more indulgent dinners. You can also do healthier swaps – if you don't want to add cream to a recipe then swap for a low-fat alternative (although don't boil the sauces because lower fat creams are more likely to split) and swap butter for olive oil if you prefer. Obviously, we all need a treat now and then and one of the best-known mood boosters is, of course, chocolate. I've included a couple of my favourite chocolate recipes for you – including a rather delightful Rich Chocolate & Espresso Cheesecake… yum!

When talking about food and our mood I really should include the actual cooking process. I want you to enjoy cooking – there's no point in serving up tasty food if the chef is stressed and grumpy at the table! It's always best to read through the recipe first, prep ahead and have all of your ingredients out ready in front of you before you start. If the list of ingredients is slightly long, it always helps to have everything measured out so that you can work in order rather than stopping to look for a spice at the back of the cupboard while the onions burn. I'm also well aware that peeling and chopping an onion takes much longer than we think it will, especially when you have kids or pets interrupting you (yes, Bobby, that means you!). If you don't feel like mincing or grating garlic, then buy a garlic press – they're so easy to use (although not quite so easy to clean!). If there's a lot of chopping involved, use your food processor – I often use mine for coleslaw as it shreds the cabbage in seconds. A good set of knives always helps to save time too – I know it sounds obvious, but it really does take so much longer to chop things if your knives aren't kept really sharp. Organise your space as best as you can – clear your area, have your knives, chopping board, any necessary equipment and a couple of utensils to hand, put on some good tunes, relax, feel the vibe and enjoy. Make the kitchen your happy place and I promise the results will speak for themselves. If the cooking is joyful it will be reflected in the food – as my mother used to say, 'the food is smiling'. Oh, and to make things easier on a busy weeknight don't worry about cheating a little – use pre-cooked rice or grains and shop-bought items such as hummus and pastry. We all do it and I've included recipes just for those moments. Or choose a one-pot or a traybake. Quick and easy one-pot dishes using simple ingredients are a foolproof and fuss-free way of feeding the family with little waste. You also save on a lot of washing up, which is never a bad thing!

It's been pretty difficult to narrow down my good mood food – I love such a variety! So I've included a selection of my favourite dishes for you: food that I loved as a child, dishes that remind me of home, some that I've enjoyed making for and with my kids over the years and a few of my favourite meals from my travels. Basically, food that makes me happy! There are comforting classics you'll be familiar with – you can't beat a Beer-Battered Fish with Triple-Cooked Chips & Minty Mushy Peas or a comforting Baked Vanilla & Ginger Custard; food that's great for sharing – dig into my Spicy Three Bean & Pepper Chilli Pot; recipes for a bit of indulgence – enjoy my Slow-Braised Lamb Shanks in Red Wine with Rosemary, Garlic & Anchovies; light and healthy dishes to make you feel good from the inside – try my Smoked Salmon Super Salad with Dill & Turmeric Dressing; quick and easy one-pots – my Easy Sausage, Bacon & Bean Bake is definitely a mid-week winner and, of course, some of my favourite barbecue dishes to bring some sunshine to your plate – my vibrant Chargrilled Chicken & Pineapple Chow Skewers with Fresh Coconut Slaw will certainly brighten up your day. I hope you enjoy the recipes as much as I do and that they soon become your good mood food too. Happy cooking everyone, and don't forget to share your finished dishes with me over on Instagram @ainsleyfoods #ainsleysgoodmoodfood.

Chapter One
LIGHT BITES

Breakfast Hash with 'Nduja & Kale

This tasty hash is perfect for a hearty weekend breakfast or brunch. The combination of potatoes, peppers and kale is spiced up with 'nduja, a spreadable Italian sausage that really packs a punch, so you only need a little to add a lovely smoky kick (try it on my Pizza Margherita on page 91). You can swap it with spicy chorizo or, of course, you can leave it out for a veggie hash – just add a pinch of smoked paprika in with the garlic for flavour.

SERVES 4

2–3 large Yukon Gold or red potatoes, peeled and cut into small chunks
1 large sweet potato, peeled and cut into small chunks
140g curly kale, tough stems removed, chopped
1 tbsp olive oil
1 onion, chopped
1 red pepper, de-seeded and cut into strips or chunks
1 garlic clove, minced
1 tbsp butter
50g 'nduja
4 eggs
a handful of flat-leaf parsley, chopped (optional)
sea salt and freshly ground black pepper

Place the potatoes in a saucepan and cover with boiling water. Add a good pinch of salt and bring to the boil, then simmer for 3 minutes. Add the sweet potato then simmer for a further 3 minutes. Drain well, leaving them in the colander to steam dry.

Blanch the kale in a large pan of boiling salted water for 1 minute. Drain well, refresh in cold water and drain again. Squeeze out any excess water and set aside.

Meanwhile, heat the oil in a large non-stick frying pan that has a lid over a medium heat. Add the onion and pepper and sauté for 4–6 minutes until softened. Add the garlic and cook for another 30 seconds until fragrant.

Add the butter and, once it is foaming, tip in the potatoes, season well with salt and pepper and stir to coat in the butter. Sauté over a medium-high heat for 8–10 minutes until they are crisp and golden.

Dot over pieces of the 'nduja and continue to sauté for another minute, pressing down with the back of a spoon to crisp everything up. Stir in the kale and check the seasoning. Make 4 wells in the vegetables and crack an egg into each. Cover and cook over a low-medium heat until the eggs are cooked to your liking.

Season the eggs with salt and pepper, and scatter over the parsley (if using) to serve.

Cheese & Greens Breakfast Muffins

The smell of these breakfast muffins baking in the morning is delightful. They're truly moreish and, of course, they're actually good for any time of the day. Delicious with soup and perfect for picnics, these are also a great way to get your kids to eat some greens. You can really mix up the greens too – when in season I love to throw in a handful of wild garlic, or a mix of spinach and watercress is nice as it adds a peppery twist. As a treat, sometimes I swap the seeds on top for a little crispy bacon.

MAKES 12 MUFFINS

150g baby spinach leaves (or a mix of your favourite soft green leaves)
1 egg, beaten
300ml milk
50g butter, melted
1 heaped tsp English mustard
350g plain flour
2 tsp baking powder
½ tsp caster sugar
1 tsp salt
2 tsp finely snipped chives
100g Cheddar or Gruyère, grated
1 tbsp pumpkin or sunflower seeds

Preheat the oven to 200°C/180°C fan/gas 6. Line a 12-hole muffin tin with paper cases.

Put the spinach in a sieve or colander and slowly pour over a full kettle of boiling water. Refresh under cold water then squeeze out all of the moisture, using your hands. Add to a food processor and blitz until finely chopped. Add the egg, milk, melted butter and mustard and blend until well combined.

Sift the flour and baking powder into a large bowl and stir in the sugar, salt, chives and three quarters of the grated cheese.

Stir the liquid into the dry ingredients, taking care not to over-mix – it should be evenly distributed but still quite lumpy. Divide the mixture between the muffin cases, scatter over the remaining grated cheese and the seeds and bake for 18–20 minutes until golden, firm and a skewer inserted into the centre comes out clean.

Transfer to a wire rack and allow to cool slightly. Delicious when served warm.

Tropical Green Smoothie

This smoothie is full of green goodness and tropical zing, and I love the hint of ginger which gives a little kick and a healthy boost to the digestive system. It makes for a refreshing and vibrant start to the day. You can use coconut or almond milk instead of the coconut water if you want a creamier smoothie, and swap the avocado for a banana if you prefer.

SERVES 2

1 x 230g tin pineapple chunks in juice (or fresh pineapple and 2–3 tbsp juice)
1 large mango, peeled, stoned and chopped
1 avocado, peeled, stoned and roughly chopped
1 tsp chia seeds (optional)
100g baby spinach leaves
330–350ml chilled unsweetened coconut water
4cm piece of fresh root ginger, peeled and grated
6–8 mint leaves, torn
1–2 tbsp honey or maple syrup (optional; to taste)

Put the pineapple chunks and their juice, the mango, avocado, chia seeds (if using) and spinach into a high-speed blender and pour over 330ml coconut water. Add the ginger and mint and blend until smooth. Taste for sweetness and add a little honey or maple syrup if required. If it is too thick, add a dash more coconut water and pulse again.

Pour into chilled glasses and enjoy!

Brioche French Toast with Orange & Honey-roasted Figs, Hazelnuts & Mascarpone

This is one of my favourite flavour combinations and it's an absolute treat for a lazy Sunday brunch. The sticky, luscious figs and earthy hazelnuts are sublime with the rich and decadent French toast – or as I like to call it, naughty eggy bread! You can enjoy the toast and figs with yoghurt instead of mascarpone if you want to be a little less naughty.

SERVES 4

250g mascarpone
zest and juice of
    1 large orange
140ml single cream
6 ripe figs, halved
    lengthways
2 tsp butter, plus
    extra for frying
2 tbsp runny honey,
    plus extra (optional)
    for drizzling
30g blanched hazelnuts,
    roughly chopped
3 large eggs
½ tsp vanilla bean paste
    or extract
1 heaped tbsp golden
    caster sugar
4–6 thick slices (about
    2.5cm thick) of brioche
icing sugar, for dusting
    (optional)

Preheat the oven to 200°C/180°C fan/gas 6. Line a baking tray with baking parchment or foil.

In a bowl, whisk together the mascarpone and half the orange zest and juice. Add a splash of the cream if it needs loosening a little (or for a treat add a splash of Cointreau!). Cover and chill until needed.

Place the figs on the lined baking tray, cut-side up, and dot with a little butter. Drizzle the honey over the figs and squeeze over the remaining orange juice. Scatter over the hazelnuts and roast for 14–16 minutes or until the figs have softened and caramelised and the nuts are nice and golden. Remove from the oven and turn off the heat.

In a large shallow dish, whisk the eggs with the cream. Add the vanilla, remaining orange zest and sugar and whisk again until well combined.

Melt a knob of butter in a large frying pan over a medium heat. Dip each slice of brioche into the egg mixture, letting it soak up the liquid for a few seconds before turning over to coat the other side. Once the butter is foaming, add the soaked brioche to the pan one or two at a time and cook for 2–3 minutes on each side until golden brown and crisp. Transfer to a wire rack in the still-warm oven while you cook the remaining slices, adding a little more butter to the pan if needed.

To serve, slice the French toast in half and place 2–3 pieces on each serving plate. Top with 3 halves of the sticky figs, drizzling over any roasting juices, and a little extra drizzle of honey if you like. Add a spoonful of the mascarpone and dust with icing sugar, if using, to serve.

Carrot & Cardamom Courgette Fritters with Mango Chutney Yoghurt

These vegan and gluten-free vegetable fritters are fantastic for a delicious brunch or light lunch, and I cook them often for family and friends. The fruity, sweet and spicy yoghurt makes a lovely accompaniment.

MAKES 8 FRITTERS

2 large courgettes (about 450g in total), coarsely grated
½ tsp salt
1 large carrot (about 150g), coarsely grated
60g gram (chickpea) flour, plus extra if needed
½ tsp gluten-free baking powder
2 tbsp chopped coriander or flat-leaf parsley
1 tsp snipped chives, plus extra to serve
seeds of 3–4 cardamom pods, crushed
¼ tsp ground turmeric
zest of ½ lemon
freshly ground black pepper
groundnut or sunflower oil, for frying

For the mango chutney yoghurt
1 tbsp good-quality mango chutney
a dash of hot pepper sauce (optional)
150g thick coconut yoghurt

First, make the mango chutney yoghurt. In a small bowl, swirl the mango chutney and hot pepper sauce (if using) through the yoghurt, cover and chill until needed.

Place the grated courgette in a sieve over a bowl, stir in the salt and set aside for 8–10 minutes. Using your hands, squeeze out any moisture from the courgettes and put them into a clean, dry bowl with the grated carrot. Stir in the flour, baking powder, chopped herbs, cardamom, turmeric and lemon zest and season generously with pepper. Stir well to combine into a thick batter mixture. Adjust the flour accordingly – it will depend on the size of your vegetables.

Heat 2 tablespoons of oil in a large non-stick frying pan over a medium heat. Once hot, add 4 heaped spoonfuls of the batter, making sure they're spaced well apart and using the tip of the spoon to create a nice round shape. Cook for 2–3 minutes without moving until golden underneath, then carefully turn to cook the other side for 2–3 minutes until crisp on the outside and cooked through. Remove from the pan, place on kitchen paper to drain and keep warm while you make the remaining fritters, adding a little more oil to the pan if needed.

Serve the fritters topped with a dollop of the mango chutney yoghurt and sprinkled with snipped chives.

Chargrilled Asparagus with Ham Hock & Pleasing Pea Salad

This is a super-easy and flavourful salad using prepared ham hock that's readily available in supermarkets. I love the saltiness of the ham with fresh, sweet peas – it's a classic combination and very pleasing indeed! Perfect for a light lunch, but if you want a more substantial meal, add a few cooked new potatoes.

SERVES 2

2 eggs
150g fine asparagus
    spears, trimmed
olive oil, for drizzling
120g fresh podded peas
    (or use frozen, defrosted)
120g sugar snap peas,
    halved lengthways
4–6 radishes, trimmed
    and finely sliced
2 spring onions, trimmed
    and finely sliced
2 tbsp roughly chopped
    fresh tarragon
1 small bunch of mint,
    leaves picked and
    shredded
a small bag (about 60g)
    of pea shoots
a large handful of peppery
    leaves (watercress,
    mustard or rocket)
1 x 180g pack shredded
    or pulled ham hock
sea salt and freshly
    ground black pepper

For the dressing
1 tbsp cider vinegar or
    white wine vinegar
3 tbsp rapeseed or
    light olive oil
1 tsp English mustard

Bring a medium pan of water to a gentle simmer, add the eggs and boil for 6–8 minutes, depending on your preference. Drain and run them under cold water for 2 minutes. When cool enough to handle, peel and set aside.

Meanwhile, put the asparagus into a bowl and drizzle with a little olive oil. Toss to coat. Heat a griddle pan over a medium heat and, when hot, add the asparagus spears. Cook for 2–3 minutes, turning occasionally, until lightly charred and tender. Remove from the heat and sprinkle with a little salt. Set aside.

Bring another pan of water to the boil, add the peas, cook for 2 minutes then drain well and refresh in a bowl of ice-cold water.

In a small bowl, whisk all the ingredients for the dressing together and season.

Drain the peas well, patting them dry with kitchen paper if needed, and place in a large bowl with the sliced sugar snap peas. Stir in a third of the dressing. Add the radish, spring onion, tarragon and mint and toss through the pea shoots and salad leaves. Drizzle over a little more dressing and then arrange on a serving platter. Scatter the chargrilled asparagus and ham hock on top. Cut the eggs into halves or quarters and add to the salad. Season and drizzle over the remaining dressing, if needed. Serve immediately with some crusty bread.

Baked Garlic Portobello Mushrooms Stuffed with Hummus & Herby Breadcrumbs

I love garlic mushrooms and they're great for a tasty brunch or light meal. Filling them with hummus may sound a little strange, but trust me, it's delightful! A simple salad is the perfect accompaniment, or sometimes just a slice of sourdough toast on the side is enough. The exact amount of hummus and breadcrumbs you need will depend on the size of your mushrooms, so do adjust accordingly.

SERVES 4

4 large Portobello or flat field mushrooms, wiped clean
2 garlic cloves, finely chopped
a pinch of pul biber or chilli flakes
1½ tbsp extra-virgin olive oil, plus extra for drizzling
50g fresh breadcrumbs
2 tbsp pine nuts
2 tbsp finely chopped fresh herbs (I like parsley, chives and dill), plus extra to serve
8 tbsp good-quality hummus
a small bag (about 60g) of mixed baby salad leaves
a handful of cherry tomatoes, halved
balsamic glaze (optional)
sea salt and freshly ground black pepper

Preheat the oven to 200°C/180°C fan/gas 6.

Remove the stems from the mushrooms and set aside. Place the mushrooms in a small baking tray or dish and sprinkle each one with the garlic and pul biber. Drizzle over a little olive oil and season with salt and pepper. Cover loosely with foil and bake for 10–12 minutes.

Meanwhile, finely chop the mushroom stems and put them in a bowl along with the breadcrumbs, pine nuts, chopped herbs and olive oil. Mix well and season.

Remove the mushrooms from the oven and spoon 1–2 tablespoons of hummus into each mushroom (depending on the size of your mushrooms). Top each with the breadcrumb mixture. Return to the oven, uncovered, for 10–12 minutes or until the breadcrumbs are golden and crispy.

Meanwhile, put the salad leaves and tomatoes into a bowl and drizzle with a little olive oil. Season with a pinch of salt and toss to coat. Drizzle with a little balsamic glaze (if using) and serve the mushrooms hot and scattered with fresh herbs, with the salad on the side.

Spiced Roast Parsnip & Coconut Soup

I love making soup with roasted vegetables because you get a much richer flavour. This easy traybake parsnip soup has a lovely delicate curry taste that's really comforting. It works well with other root vegetables too, so feel free to mix it up. This is a light and vegan-friendly soup, but if you prefer a creamier consistency just stir in a little coconut cream or double cream at the end of cooking.

SERVES 4–6

750g parsnips,
    peeled and cubed
4 large garlic cloves, peeled
1 onion, peeled and cut
    into 8 wedges
3cm piece of fresh root
    ginger, peeled and
    roughly chopped
1½ tbsp olive oil
½ tsp fennel seeds
1 tbsp mild curry powder
1–1.2 litres vegetable
    stock, hot
1 x 400ml tin coconut milk
1 tbsp finely chopped
    coriander, plus extra
    to garnish
sea salt and freshly
    ground black pepper
coconut flakes, toasted,
    to serve (optional)

Preheat the oven to 200°C/180°C fan/gas 6.

Place the parsnip, garlic, onion and ginger in a large, deep roasting tin. Drizzle over the oil then sprinkle over the fennel seeds and curry powder. Season with salt and pepper and toss everything together to coat. Roast for 25 minutes until lightly golden.

Pour 500ml of the stock and all the coconut milk into the roasting tin and return to the oven for a further 20–25 minutes until the vegetables are tender.

Carefully transfer the contents of the roasting tin to a food processor and blend until smooth. Add the remaining stock until you reach the desired consistency. Add the chopped coriander and check for seasoning. If necessary, warm through again before serving.

Ladle into warm bowls, scatter with extra coriander and toasted coconut flakes (if using). Serve with fresh crusty bread.

Date & Walnut Bread

There's something very pleasing and comforting about the smell of home-baked bread, and this loaf smells and tastes wonderful. I love the textures of the crunchy walnuts and the sweet sticky dates. It's delicious spread with just butter or try it with a creamy blue cheese and an aromatic honey. I like to use a combination of plain and wholemeal flour but this also works well with just white flour if you want a milder loaf (reduce the yeast to 7g).

MAKES 2 SMALL LOAVES

350g strong white flour, plus extra for dusting
200g strong wholemeal flour
1 rounded tsp salt
50g butter, diced
10g fast-action dried yeast
350ml tepid water
olive oil, for greasing
85g soft dates, pitted and roughly chopped
80g walnuts, roughly chopped

Put the flours and salt into a large bowl. Using your fingertips, rub in the butter until the mixture resembles fine breadcrumbs. Stir in the yeast until well combined.

Make a well in the centre of the dry ingredients then gradually pour in the water while mixing to combine to a soft, pliable dough. Turn out onto a lightly floured work surface and knead for 10 minutes until smooth and elastic. Place in an oiled bowl, cover and leave to rise in a warm place for about 1 hour, until doubled in size.

Gently deflate and knock back the dough, then mix in the dates and walnuts until evenly distributed.

Divide the dough in half and shape each piece into an oval. Place on a non-stick baking sheet (or two baking sheets if small) and cover each one with a damp tea towel. If using one baking sheet, ensure that there is enough space between the loaves to allow for expansion. Leave to rise again in a warm place for 45 minutes.

Preheat the oven to 220°C/200°C fan/gas 7.

Slash the tops of the loaves with a sharp knife and bake for 10 minutes, then reduce the oven temperature to 190°C/170°C fan/gas 5 and bake for a further 25–30 minutes until the loaves sound hollow when tapped on the bottom.

Transfer to a wire rack to cool completely – if you can wait that long!

Salt & Pepper Calamari with a Hot & Sour Dipping Sauce

Calamari has always been one of my favourite nibbles. It's quick and easy to make at home and here I've added a light crisp coating and the flavours of the classic Chinese takeaway favourite, salt and pepper squid. The hot and sour dipping sauce is optional, but I think it adds a lovely piquancy.

SERVES 4

2 tsp black peppercorns
1 tbsp Sichuan peppercorns
1 tbsp flaky sea salt
100g cornflour
100g plain flour
sunflower or vegetable oil,
    for deep-frying and frying
750g fresh baby squid,
    cleaned and cut into 1cm
    rings, tentacles left intact
3 spring onions, trimmed
    and finely sliced
2 red chillies, de-seeded and
    finely sliced into rings
2 garlic cloves, sliced
a handful of coriander
    leaves, to garnish
lemon wedges, to serve
    (optional)

For the dipping sauce
juice of 2–3 limes
2–3 tbsp soft light brown
    sugar or caster sugar
1 red chilli, de-seeded and
    finely chopped
1½ tbsp fish sauce
1 tbsp finely chopped
    coriander

In a dry frying pan over a medium heat, toast all the peppercorns for 30–60 seconds until fragrant. Tip into a pestle and mortar along with the salt and crush to a coarse powder.

Mix the cornflour and plain flour with half of the pepper mix in a large shallow bowl, then set aside. Line a tray or large plate with kitchen paper.

Make the dipping sauce. In a small bowl, mix together the juice of 2 limes and 2 tablespoons of sugar until the sugar has dissolved. Balance for sweet and sour with more lime or sugar if needed. Stir in the chilli, fish sauce and coriander and set aside.

Heat about a 7cm depth of oil in a deep-fryer or deep, heavy-based saucepan to 180°C. If you don't have a thermometer, test by dropping in a small piece of bread – it should brown in 15–20 seconds. Toss the squid in the flour mixture until well coated, shake off the excess then deep-fry in batches for about 2 minutes or until lightly golden and crisp. Use a slotted spoon to lift out the squid, then drain on the kitchen paper.

Meanwhile, heat a good drizzle of oil in a wok or large frying pan and add the spring onions and chilli. Stir-fry for 30 seconds then add the garlic. Cook for a further 30 seconds, stirring to prevent burning. Add the squid and toss to combine all the flavours. Sprinkle with a little more of the pepper mix and transfer everything to a serving plate. Scatter with coriander leaves and a little more seasoning if required. Serve immediately with the dipping sauce on the side and lemon wedges for squeezing, if you like.

Chilled Melon, Tomato & Halloumi Salad with Serrano Ham

A wonderfully simple, colourful and vibrant salad that's great for summer dining or as a refreshing starter. I love the subtle sweet and nutty saltiness of Spanish Serrano ham but you can use prosciutto if you prefer as they're quite similar. The soft meat pairs wonderfully with the salty grilled cheese, chilled sweet melon and touch of smoky paprika. This salad also works well with burrata or shavings of Manchego cheese if you fancy a change from the grilled halloumi.

SERVES 4

3 tbsp extra-virgin olive oil,
   plus extra for brushing
1 tbsp sherry vinegar
   or red wine vinegar
2 tsp runny honey
   or maple syrup
juice of ½ orange
300g heirloom tomatoes
   (mix of colour and sizes),
   chopped into chunks
   and slices
500g chilled mixed melon
   (watermelon, cantaloupe)
   peeled, de-seeded and
   cut into chunks
8–12 slices of Serrano ham
1 x 250g pack halloumi,
   cut into 8 slices
sweet smoked paprika,
   for dusting
a handful of basil leaves,
   some shredded
8–10 mint leaves, shredded
flaky sea salt and freshly
   ground black pepper

In a small bowl, whisk together the oil, vinegar, honey and a good squeeze of the orange juice.

Place the tomatoes and melon in a bowl and toss with a little of the dressing. Arrange on a serving platter with the slices of ham.

Heat a ridged griddle pan or frying pan over a medium-high heat and brush with a little oil. Sprinkle the halloumi with a little paprika and cook for 1–2 minutes on each side until golden. Squeeze over a little orange juice and remove from the heat.

Season the tomatoes and melon with a pinch of flaky sea salt (not too much because the cheese and ham are salty) and a grind of pepper. Scatter over the herbs and top with the griddled halloumi. Drizzle with dressing and sprinkle over a little pinch of paprika. Serve immediately.

Butternut Squash, Stilton & Pecan Pastry Rolls

These puff pastry veggie rolls are filled with a delicious combination of sweet and nutty butternut squash, earthy sage and sharp blue cheese. They're great for picnics or just as a tasty snack. If you're not a fan of blue cheese, try using feta – I find them yummy either way!

MAKES 8 ROLLS

850g butternut squash, peeled, de-seeded and cut into 2cm chunks
olive oil, for drizzling
a pinch of chilli flakes
½ red onion, finely chopped
1 small garlic clove, minced
1 tbsp chopped sage leaves (or thyme, if you prefer)
1 tbsp finely chopped flat-leaf parsley
¼ tsp ground nutmeg
50g pecans or walnuts, roughly chopped
75g Stilton or similar hard blue cheese, crumbled
1 x 320g sheet ready-made puff pastry
plain flour, for dusting
1 egg, beaten with a dash of milk
½ tsp nigella seeds
sea salt and freshly ground black pepper

Preheat the oven to 200°C/180°C fan/gas 6. Line a baking tray with baking parchment and set aside.

Put the squash chunks into a roasting tray and drizzle with a little oil. Sprinkle over the chilli flakes, toss to coat and roast for 30–35 minutes or until tender. Remove and set aside to cool.

Meanwhile, heat a little drizzle of oil in a small frying pan over a low to medium heat and cook the onion for 4 minutes until slightly softened. Add the garlic and sage and cook for another 30 seconds until fragrant. Remove from the heat and set aside to cool.

Place the cooked squash in a bowl, leaving any oil behind in the tray, and add the parsley, nutmeg and cooled onion mixture. Use a fork to lightly crush the squash pieces, leaving some lumps for texture. Fold through the chopped nuts and crumbled cheese. Season well with salt and pepper.

Unroll the pastry sheet on a lightly floured work surface and cut in half lengthways into two long strips. Divide the squash mixture in half and spoon it down the middle of each length of pastry. Roll the pastry around the filling to make a long sausage shape. Brush the seam edge with the beaten egg and press lightly to seal the join. Place join-side down and cut each roll into 4 even lengths.

Transfer to the lined baking tray. Brush the tops with the beaten egg. Use a sharp knife to score the top of each pastry and scatter with nigella seeds. Bake for 20–25 minutes until golden brown. These are delicious served hot or cold.

Crispy Cauliflower Bites with a Kickin' Korean Sauce

This fiery and tangy sauce is packed full of flavour and makes the perfect finger-licking accompaniment to my crispy cauliflower bites. Gochujang is a Korean chilli paste that's available in most supermarkets or world food stores. It's really worth getting your hands on some as it's a really versatile paste, but if not you can use your favourite hot chilli sauce. I've baked my vegan cauliflower bites for a healthier snack, but you can deep-fry for extra crunch.

SERVES 4

100g plain flour
125ml plant-based milk
2 tsp Gochujang paste
a pinch of chilli flakes
    (optional)
1 tsp garlic powder
125g panko breadcrumbs
2 tbsp sesame seeds
1 large cauliflower (about
    950g), broken into florets
sea salt and freshly
    ground black pepper
2 spring onions, trimmed
    and finely sliced, to serve

For the kickin' Korean sauce
1 tbsp coconut oil
    (or plant-based butter)
3 tbsp Gochujang paste
3 tbsp tomato ketchup
1 garlic clove, minced
juice of 1 orange
2 tbsp rice vinegar or
    white wine vinegar
2 tbsp light soy sauce
3 tbsp maple syrup

Preheat the oven to 220°C/200°C fan/gas 7. Line a baking tray with baking parchment.

In a bowl, combine the flour, milk, Gochujang paste, chilli flakes (if using), garlic powder and a good pinch each of salt and black pepper. Whisk until well combined into a thick batter.

Put the breadcrumbs, sesame seeds and a small pinch of salt into a shallow dish.

Dip a cauliflower floret into the Gochujang batter and then toss in the breadcrumbs and sesame, until fully coated. Place on the lined baking tray. Repeat with the remaining florets.

Bake for 25–30 minutes until golden brown and crispy, turning the cauliflower pieces after 20 minutes.

Meanwhile, melt the coconut oil in a saucepan over a medium heat. Stir in the remaining sauce ingredients and bring to the boil. Stir well until smooth then remove from the heat. Season and adjust for sweetness.

When the cauliflower bites are cooked, place on a serving platter and scatter over the spring onions. Serve immediately with the kickin' sauce for dipping.

Fruity Oat Energy Bars

These fruity oat bars are moreish and nutritious and certain to give you a boost of feel-good energy. By using coconut oil they can easily be suitable for vegans and you can choose your favourite combination of dried fruit, nuts and seeds. They're great for a grab-and-go breakfast, lunchboxes or an afternoon snack and, best of all, kids love them.

MAKES 12 BARS

50g butter or coconut oil, plus extra for greasing
125g ready-chopped dates or ready-to-eat dried apricots, chopped
125ml orange juice
100g demerara sugar
80g maple syrup or runny honey
a small pinch of sea salt
180g jumbo porridge oats
1 tsp ground cinnamon
25g sesame seeds
50g mixture of sunflower and pumpkin seeds
25g desiccated coconut
40g mixture of sultanas, cranberries and dried cherries
80g mixture of pecans, almonds and peanuts, roughly chopped

Preheat the oven to 190°C/170°C fan/gas 5. Grease a 20 x 20cm baking tin and line with baking parchment.

Put the dates or apricots and orange juice into a medium saucepan and bring to the boil. Reduce the heat and simmer gently for 4–5 minutes, stirring occasionally, or until the dates have completely softened. You should have a nice thick purée – if using apricots you may need to transfer to a mini food processor to blend then tip back into the pan. Add the butter, sugar, maple syrup and salt and heat gently, stirring, over a low-medium heat for 3–4 minutes until melted and the sugar has dissolved.

Remove from the heat, stir in the remaining ingredients and mix until well combined, ensuring all the oats are coated.

Tip into the prepared baking tin and press down in an even layer with the back of a spoon or a spatula. Bake for about 20 minutes or until golden. Leave to cool in the tin, cutting it into 12 bars while still just warm.

Roasted Beetroot, Candied Walnut & Goat's Cheese Salad

Earthy beetroot works so well with salty and creamy goat's cheese and it's a classic flavour combination that I never tire of. I've used a selection of different coloured beetroot, which looks really pretty on the plate, and cooked and raw beets for added texture, but you can stick with purple beetroot if that's all you can get hold of. Serve with fresh crusty bread.

SERVES 4

4–6 medium-sized purple beetroot, scrubbed and trimmed
2–4 medium-sized heritage or candy beetroot, trimmed and peeled
25g caster sugar
1 tsp butter
a pinch of chilli flakes (optional)
60g walnut halves, toasted
150g goat's cheese, crumbled
6–8 mint leaves, shredded
a handful of lamb's lettuce or watercress
zest of ½ orange
flaky sea salt and freshly ground black pepper

For the dressing
2 tbsp walnut oil
1 tbsp extra-virgin olive oil
1½ tbsp sherry vinegar or red wine vinegar
1 tsp Dijon mustard or horseradish
2 tsp runny honey
zest and juice of ½ orange

Preheat the oven to 200°C/180°C fan/gas 6.

Place the purple beetroot in a roasting tin and add about a 6mm depth of water. Cover the tin tightly with foil and roast for 40–50 minutes or until tender. Leave to cool, then use your fingers (you may want to wear gloves!) or kitchen paper to rub the skins from the beetroot. Cut into wedges.

Meanwhile, cut the heritage or candy beetroot into very thin slices, using either a mandoline or a very sharp knife. Put into a bowl.

In a small bowl, whisk together the dressing ingredients. Lightly season and pour half over the thinly sliced raw beetroot. Leave to marinate for 30 minutes while the purple beetroot is roasting.

Line a baking sheet with baking parchment. Place the sugar, butter and chilli flakes (if using) in a small non-stick frying pan and cook over a medium heat, stirring, until the butter and sugar have melted and turned lightly golden. Stir in the walnuts for a minute until the nuts are nicely coated. Pour out onto the lined baking sheet and use two forks to quickly separate the nuts. Sprinkle with a little sea salt and leave to cool completely.

To serve, arrange the thinly sliced discs of marinated beetroot on a plate then pile the wedges of roasted beetroot on top. Scatter over the goat's cheese, mint and candied walnuts and top with salad leaves. Sprinkle over some orange zest, drizzle over the remaining dressing and season with a little flaky sea salt.

Chicken & Chickpea Roti Wraps

Bring the sunshine into your kitchen with these tasty wraps. Roti filled with delicious curries are a popular street food in the Caribbean – there's nothing better than picking one up from a beach shack vendor, sitting on the beach and watching the sun go down while enjoying your tasty snack and sipping on a rum punch! If you fancy a veggie roti, just swap the chicken for 500g of pumpkin or squash chunks.

SERVES 4

2 tbsp coconut oil
    or light olive oil
1 red onion, thinly sliced
3 garlic cloves, minced
½ Scotch bonnet chilli,
    de-seeded and
    finely chopped
4–5 skinless and boneless
    chicken thighs (or 2
    breasts), trimmed and
    cut into bite-sized pieces
1 x 400g tin chickpeas,
    drained and rinsed
1 heaped tbsp Caribbean
    curry powder
½ tsp ground turmeric
1 tsp ground cumin
1 tsp sea salt
60ml water
150ml coconut milk
1 tsp chopped fresh
    thyme leaves
1 tsp maple syrup
½ lime, for squeezing
a handful of coriander
    leaves, chopped,
    plus extra to serve
natural yoghurt and hot
    pepper sauce, to serve

For the roti
225g plain flour, plus
    extra for dusting
½ tsp salt
1 tsp baking powder
200ml water
melted butter or light
    olive oil, for brushing

First, make the roti. In a large bowl, sift together the flour, salt and baking powder. Gradually add the water, mixing with your hands until the mixture forms a dough. You may need more or less water – the dough should be pliable and soft, yet firm. Cover the dough with a clean tea towel and leave to rest for 20–30 minutes.

Meanwhile, put a deep-sided frying pan over a medium heat and add 1 tablespoon of the oil. Add the onion and cook for 4–6 minutes until softened but not coloured, then add the garlic and chilli and cook for 30 seconds. Remove the onion mixture from the pan using a slotted spoon. Add the remaining oil over a medium-high heat and, when hot, add the chicken. Cook, stirring, for 3–4 minutes or until lightly browned. Reduce the heat, stir in the chickpeas, curry powder, turmeric, cumin and salt, and toss to combine. Cook for a minute. Stir in the water and cook for 2–3 minutes until it has evaporated. Return the onion mixture to the pan and stir in the coconut milk, thyme and maple syrup. Cook over a medium heat for a few more minutes until the chicken is cooked through. Check for seasoning, stir in lime juice to taste, and the coriander.

When the dough has rested, knead on a lightly floured work surface until smooth. Divide into 4 equal balls, flatten slightly and roll out into rounds 20–23cm in diameter and 5mm thick. Brush with melted butter or oil, fold in half, then fold into quarters, roll back into balls, and roll out again into 20–23cm rounds.

Heat a dry, heavy-based frying pan or flat griddle over a medium heat. Brush each roti with a little more butter or oil and add one or two at a time to the pan. Cook for 3–4 minutes until browned bubbles appear, turning occasionally and brushing with butter or oil each time you do. Remove from the pan, wrap in a clean tea towel and keep the roti warm while you cook the rest.

Divide the chicken between the roti, scatter over the coriander and drizzle with yoghurt and a dash of hot sauce. Wrap up and enjoy!

Chapter Two

VEGGIE & VEGAN

Roasted Butternut Squash & Garlic Risotto

A silky risotto is a wonderful meal and although they take a bit of care during cooking they're surprisingly easy to make with very few ingredients. I love the creaminess of this dish and the roasting of the squash and garlic adds a fabulous richness. For a nice garnish, try frying some sage leaves in a little olive oil to serve on top of the finished dish.

SERVES 4

500g butternut squash, peeled, de-seeded and cut into 1.5cm dice
5–6 garlic cloves, unpeeled
1 tbsp chopped sage leaves
3 tbsp olive oil
60g butter
1 onion, finely chopped
300g arborio risotto rice
80ml dry white wine
1–1.4 litres vegetable stock, hot
2 tbsp chopped flat-leaf parsley
60g vegetarian Italian hard cheese (Parmesan if non-vegetarian), grated
extra-virgin olive oil, for drizzling
sea salt and freshly ground black pepper

Preheat the oven to 220°C/200°C fan/gas 7.

Place the squash, garlic and half the sage leaves in a shallow roasting tin and drizzle with 2 tablespoons of the olive oil. Season with salt, toss to coat and roast for 25–30 minutes until tender and caramelised.

Meanwhile, heat the remaining oil and half the butter in a large deep-sided frying pan over a medium heat. When the butter has melted, add the onion and cook for 4–6 minutes until softened but not coloured. Add the rice, stir and toast for 2–3 minutes until translucent. Pour in the wine, stirring while it evaporates.

Add the remaining sage leaves and season with black pepper. Stir to combine. Add the stock a little at a time, ensuring that the liquid is absorbed before adding any more. Stir through, continuing to cook at a medium simmer, stirring continuously, and adding the stock little by little for about 20 minutes.

Remove the squash from the oven and take out the garlic and set aside. Mash two thirds of the squash with a potato masher, leaving some texture, and stir this through the risotto. Squeeze the garlic from their skins and then stir through the risotto, along with the parsley.

Check that the rice is cooked to your liking – it should be soft but still with a nutty bite. Remove from the heat and stir through the remaining butter and half the cheese. Check for seasoning – you shouldn't need much, if any, salt because of the cheese. Serve immediately, topped with the remaining chunks of butternut squash, a drizzle of extra-virgin olive oil and the remaining grated cheese.

Sautéed Fennel, Courgette & Broad Beans with Creamy Polenta & Herb Dressing

This recipe is dreamy – gently caramelised fennel with fresh green vegetables and herbs served on a bed of creamy and comforting polenta. Veggie heaven! If you have larger broad beans or they're just podded then it's worth blanching them first for a minute or two and peeling off their outer skins.

SERVES 4

1 tsp fennel seeds
60g butter
extra-virgin olive oil,
    for drizzling
1 heaped tsp caster sugar
1 large fennel bulb, cut
    into thin vertical slices,
    fronds reserved
20ml white wine
    or vermouth
1 large courgette, halved
    lengthways and sliced
3 garlic cloves, sliced
200g small broad beans
    (or defrosted frozen)
60g baby spinach leaves
8–10 fresh basil leaves,
    shredded
1 tbsp chopped flat-leaf
    parsley
zest and juice of ½ lemon
40g pine nuts, toasted
sea salt and freshly
    ground black pepper

For the polenta
500ml milk
550ml vegetable stock
1 tsp sea salt
180g polenta
75g vegetarian Italian hard
    cheese (or Parmesan if
    non-vegetarian), grated
2 tbsp butter

For the herb dressing
a handful of basil leaves
a small handful of flat-leaf
    parsley leaves
2 tsp snipped chives
zest and juice of ½ lemon
3–4 tbsp extra-virgin olive oil
¼ tsp chilli flakes

First, make the polenta. Put the milk, stock and salt into a large, heavy-based saucepan and bring to the boil. Slowly pour in the polenta in a steady stream, whisking all the time so it thickens as you go. Keep whisking for 1–2 minutes over a medium-high heat. Reduce the heat to low, cover and cook for 30 minutes, stirring occasionally to prevent it sticking, or until softened and the polenta starts to come away from the sides of the pan.

To make the herb dressing, blitz the herbs and lemon zest together in a mini food processor. Add the extra-virgin olive oil until you have a drizzling consistency. Stir in the chilli flakes and a squeeze of the lemon juice, season with salt and set aside.

Halfway through the polenta's cooking time, start to cook the vegetables. In a large deep-sided frying pan or sauté pan over a medium-high heat, toast the fennel seeds for 30 seconds until fragrant. Add the butter and a good drizzle of olive oil. When foaming, add the sugar and fennel slices and cook for 3 minutes, without moving them, until golden, then turn and cook the other side for a minute or two. Add the wine and allow to bubble for a minute. Reduce the heat to medium and add the courgette and garlic, season well with salt and pepper and cook for 3–4 minutes until the courgette starts to colour. Reduce the heat and add the beans, cover and cook for another 2–3 minutes until the vegetables are just tender but still with plenty of bite. Add the spinach, herbs and lemon zest and juice, stirring through until the spinach leaves have wilted. Check for seasoning.

Remove the polenta from the heat and add three quarters of the cheese and the butter. Stir until melted and well combined. Check the seasoning.

Divide the polenta between warm shallow serving bowls and top with the vegetables along with any cooking juices. Scatter with the remaining cheese and drizzle with the herb dressing. Sprinkle over the toasted pine nuts and reserved fennel fronds.

Sweet Potato, Spinach & Peanut Stew

This is a hearty vegan version of one of my favourite one-pots, peanut butter chicken stew. It's so simple to make and yet it's incredibly flavourful. Peanut butter is a fantastic ingredient for flavouring and thickening stews and I like to use a crunchy version so there are extra nuts in the sauce. For the series I visited the Funky Nut Company in Birkenhead and they made me a peanut butter flavoured with Scotch bonnet chilli just for this recipe – fantastic! Serve with your favourite grains or my roti (page 46).

SERVES 4–6

2 tbsp coconut or olive oil
1 red onion, roughly
    chopped
3 garlic cloves, minced
4cm piece of fresh root
    ginger, peeled and
    finely chopped
1 Scotch bonnet chilli,
    left whole (or 1 red
    chilli, finely chopped)
1 heaped tsp sweet paprika
    (unsmoked)
½ tsp ground turmeric
5 cloves, ground
2 bay leaves
700g sweet potato, peeled
    and cut into large chunks
1 red pepper, de-seeded
    and cut into chunks
1 x 227g tin chopped
    tomatoes
1 tbsp tomato purée
1 x 400g tin black-eyed peas
    or black beans, drained
    and rinsed
150g crunchy peanut butter
350–400ml vegetable stock
180g baby spinach leaves
2 tbsp chopped coriander,
    plus extra leaves
    for serving
½ lemon, for squeezing
sea salt and freshly
    ground black pepper

Heat the oil in a heavy-based lidded saucepan or Dutchie pot over a medium heat and add the onion. Cook for 4–6 minutes until softened but not coloured. Add the garlic, ginger, chilli, spices and bay leaves and cook for a further 2 minutes, adding a splash of water if needed. Add the sweet potato and red pepper and cook for 2–3 minutes to combine the flavours. Stir in the tomatoes, tomato purée, black-eyed peas, peanut butter and 350ml stock until well combined. Season to taste.

Cover the pot and gently simmer over a low-medium heat for 20–25 minutes or until the sweet potato is tender. Stir every now and then, to prevent anything sticking to the base of the pot, adding a little more stock if needed. Stir in the spinach until just wilted. Stir in the coriander then finish with a good squeeze of lemon and check the seasoning. Remove the Scotch bonnet and bay leaves before serving.

Garnish with coriander leaves and serve with your favourite grains or my roti.

Mushroom, Kale & Chestnut Pies

These great-tasting vegan pies are full of comfort and goodness. I love the texture of the chestnuts and they add a sweet and buttery flavour that goes perfectly with the meaty mushrooms and earthy kale. A nutty and creamy celeriac mash is the perfect topping.

SERVES 4

500g Maris Piper potatoes, peeled and cut into chunks
1 small celeriac (about 500g), peeled and cut into large chunks
2 tbsp vegan butter
1 tbsp plant-based milk
2½ tbsp olive oil, plus extra to drizzle
1 red onion, finely chopped
1 celery stick, finely chopped
2 tsp fresh thyme leaves or 1 tsp dried
2 garlic cloves, minced
400g mixed mushrooms (chestnut, button), wiped clean, halved or quartered
20g dried porcini mushrooms, soaked in 100ml boiling water
180g cooked chestnuts, halved or quartered
a splash of white wine (optional)
120g young kale, stems removed, shredded
250ml vegetable stock
½ lemon, for squeezing
250ml oat or soya cream
2 tbsp chopped flat-leaf parsley, plus extra to serve
nutmeg, for grating
1 tsp cornflour, mixed with 1 tbsp water
sea salt and freshly ground black pepper

Preheat the oven to 200°C/180°C fan/gas 6.

First, make the mash. Put the potatoes and celeriac in a large pan of salted boiling water and simmer for 15–18 minutes or until tender. Drain and allow to steam dry in the colander for a few minutes. Tip back into the pan and mash well with a potato masher or pass through a ricer for super-smooth mash. Beat in the butter and milk and season well with salt and pepper. Set aside.

In a sauté pan or deep-sided frying pan over a low-medium heat, add 1 tablespoon of the olive oil and cook the onion, celery and half the thyme for 6–8 minutes, until softened and lightly golden. Add the garlic and cook for 30 seconds until fragrant. Remove from the pan onto a plate and set aside.

Add the remaining oil to the pan and increase the heat to medium-high. When hot, add the fresh mushrooms, stirring and frying for 3–4 minutes until slightly browned and softened. Reduce the heat to medium, chop the porcini mushrooms and add to the frying pan, reserving their soaking liquid. Fry for a further minute.

Return the onion to the pan along with the chestnuts and cook for a minute or two. Add a splash of wine (if using) and allow to bubble for 30 seconds then stir in the kale. Add the stock, a squeeze of lemon juice and the reserved porcini water. Simmer for 2–3 minutes, stirring until combined. Stir in the cream, parsley and remaining thyme, grate in some nutmeg to taste and season generously with salt and pepper. Add the cornflour mixture, bring to the boil and stir for a minute until thickened a little. Remove from the heat and spoon into 4 individual pie dishes or a 25cm pie dish. Allow to rest for a minute or two and then pipe or spoon the mash on top.

Bake in the oven for 20–25 minutes until golden and bubbling. Serve sprinkled with chopped parsley.

Five-Spice Crispy Tofu with Sriracha Peanut Udon Noodles

This is a spicy and satisfying vegan dish that's ideal for a week-night supper – it really doesn't take long to cook once you have all the ingredients ready. If you'd prefer things a little less spicy and on the sweet side, use a sweet chilli sauce instead of the sriracha.

SERVES 4

3 tbsp low-sodium soy sauce, plus extra to season
2 tsp toasted sesame oil, plus extra to season
5cm piece of fresh root ginger, peeled and grated
1 x 280g pack extra-firm tofu, drained and pressed, cut into 2cm cubes
½ tsp five-spice powder
5 tbsp crunchy peanut butter
½ tbsp maple syrup
2–3 tsp sriracha
80–100ml vegetable stock, hot
½ lime, for squeezing

For the stir-fry and to serve
3 tbsp cornflour
½ tsp chilli flakes
½ tsp five-spice powder
a pinch of salt
2 tbsp groundnut or sunflower oil, plus extra for drizzling
3 spring onions, trimmed and finely sliced, greens and whites separated
2 red peppers, de-seeded and thinly sliced
1 red chilli, de-seeded and finely sliced into rings
450g straight-to-wok udon noodles (or noodles pre-cooked according to packet instructions)
150g bean sprouts
1 tbsp chopped peanuts, toasted
1 lime, cut into wedges
freshly ground black pepper

Put 2 tablespoons of the soy sauce, 1 teaspoon of the sesame oil and half the ginger in a bowl. Mix to combine. Pat the tofu cubes dry with kitchen paper then add to the bowl. Toss to coat, cover and leave to marinate for 10–15 minutes.

In a small saucepan over a low-medium heat, combine the remaining soy sauce, sesame oil and ginger. Stir together with the five-spice powder, peanut butter, maple syrup and sriracha. Add the stock a little at a time until you have a thick but loose sauce (use more or less depending on your peanut butter). Bring to a gentle simmer and cook for a minute to allow the flavours to infuse. Stir in lime juice to taste. Turn off the heat and cover to keep warm.

Put the cornflour, chilli flakes, five-spice powder and salt in a bowl and mix together. Remove the tofu cubes from the marinade, shaking off any excess (reserve any marinade) and add to the cornflour, tossing to coat on all sides.

Heat a wok or deep-sided frying pan over a high heat until smoking hot. Add the groundnut oil and then add the tofu, reduce the heat to medium and cook for 6–8 minutes, turning occasionally, until golden and lightly crispy on all sides. Remove and drain on kitchen paper (keep warm in a low oven, if needed).

Wipe out the wok and place over a medium heat. Add a drizzle of oil and add the spring onion whites, red pepper and half the chilli. Stir-fry for 30 seconds, then add the noodles, any leftover tofu marinade and the bean sprouts, tossing to combine. Heat through for a minute. Add the peanut sauce and toss to ensure everything is coated, adding a splash more stock if needed. Season with soy sauce, a dash of sesame oil and freshly ground black pepper.

Serve immediately in shallow bowls topped with the crispy tofu and scattered with the peanuts, spring onion greens, chilli rings and with lime wedges for squeezing.

Fragrant Carrot, Broccoli & Cashew Pilaf with Carrot & Cumin Yoghurt

A wonderful aromatic blend of spices elevates this simple rice one-pot to another level, and it's perfect for a vegan mid-week meal or as a tasty side dish.

SERVES 6

1½ large carrots, peeled
1 head of broccoli
60g unsalted cashew nuts
1 tbsp plant-based butter
1 tbsp groundnut or
   sunflower oil
1 large onion, chopped
4 cardamom pods,
   lightly bashed
1 tsp pul biber or ½ tsp
   dried chilli flakes
1 tsp cumin seeds
1 tsp coriander seeds,
   crushed
650ml vegetable stock, hot
½ tsp ground turmeric
½ tsp ground cinnamon
300g basmati rice,
   well rinsed
60g sultanas
zest and juice of ½ lemon
1 tsp nigella seeds
3 tbsp roughly chopped
   coriander
sea salt and freshly
   ground black pepper
crispy fried onions
   (shop-bought),
   to serve (optional)

*For the carrot and
   cumin yoghurt*
150ml plant-based
   or coconut yoghurt
1 small garlic clove, minced
1 tbsp finely chopped
   coriander
½ large carrot, peeled
1 tbsp groundnut
   or sunflower oil
1 tsp cumin seeds
sea salt

Preheat the oven to 200°C/180°C fan/gas 6.

Cut the carrots in half lengthways then slice into 1cm half-moons. Holding the large stem of the broccoli, grate the head using a box grater over a bowl (or blitz in a food processor). Set aside.

In a large flameproof casserole over a medium heat, toast the cashews for a minute or two. Keep an eye on them to make sure they don't burn. Remove from the pan, roughly chop and set aside.

Heat the butter and oil in the casserole over a medium heat and add the onion. Cook for 8–10 minutes until softened and lightly golden. Add the cardamom, pul biber, cumin and coriander seeds and cook for 30–60 seconds. Reduce the heat, add the sliced carrots and a splash of the stock, cover and cook for 4 minutes, stirring occasionally, until starting to soften.

Return the heat to medium, stir in the turmeric and cinnamon and then add the rice and sultanas. Stir to coat for a minute and then add the stock. Season with salt and a generous grind of black pepper. Bring to the boil and cover with a tight-fitting lid. Reduce the heat to low and gently simmer for 15 minutes. Remove from the heat and leave to stand for 5 minutes with the lid on. Remove the lid, stir in the grated broccoli, lemon zest and nigella seeds, cover again and leave to stand for another 5 minutes.

Meanwhile, put the yoghurt into a small bowl and mix in the garlic and coriander. Grate in the half carrot and season with salt. In a small frying pan, heat the oil over a medium heat. Add the cumin seeds and cook for about 30–45 seconds until sizzling and fragrant. Immediately pour the oil over the yoghurt and stir through. Check for seasoning.

Fluff the rice with a fork and stir in half the coriander and half the toasted cashew nuts. Check for seasoning and squeeze in lemon juice to taste.

Serve garnished with the remaining coriander, cashew nuts and crispy fried onions (if using). Top with dollops of the yoghurt.

Heart-Warming Vegetable & Lentil Lasagne

Everyone loves a lasagne and this veggie-packed dish will satisfy all the family – even the meat eaters. Keep the vegetables chunky for texture and mix them up if you like; I sometimes swap the aubergine for squash for a change of flavour. The recipe can easily be adapted for a vegan lasagne – just use a plant-based milk and olive oil instead of butter to make the white sauce and skip the cheese (or use a vegan alternative). Comforting home cooking at its best!

SERVES 6

3 tbsp olive oil, plus
    extra for drizzling
1 onion, finely chopped
1 large carrot,
    finely chopped
1 celery stick,
    finely chopped
2 garlic cloves, minced
1 tsp dried oregano
2 peppers (one red, one
    green), de-seeded and
    cut into 2cm chunks
1 aubergine, cut into
    2cm chunks
1 large courgette, halved
    lengthways and cut
    into 2cm slices
60ml red wine (vegetarian)
1 tbsp tomato purée
200ml vegetable stock
1 x 400g tin lentils,
    drained and rinsed
1 x 400g tin cherry
    tomatoes
6–8 basil leaves, shredded,
    plus extra to serve
300g dried lasagne sheets
40g vegetarian Italian
    hard cheese, grated
    (or Parmesan if
    non-vegetarian)
sea salt and freshly
    ground black pepper

For the bechamel
100g butter
100g plain flour
1 litre whole milk
1 bay leaf
nutmeg, for grating
salt and white pepper

Heat the oil in a deep-sided frying pan over a low-medium heat and gently cook the onion, carrot and celery with a good pinch of salt for 8–10 minutes until softened but not coloured. Add the garlic and oregano and cook for 30 seconds until fragrant. Increase the heat to medium, add the peppers, aubergine and courgette and cook for 4–6 minutes. Add the wine and cook for a couple of minutes to reduce and burn off the alcohol. Stir through the tomato purée then add the stock, lentils and tomatoes. Bring to the boil then lower the heat and simmer gently for 20–25 minutes until the vegetables are tender but still with bite. Season generously with salt and black pepper and stir in the basil leaves.

Meanwhile, make the bechamel. Melt the butter in a saucepan over a medium heat. Stir in the flour and cook, stirring, for 1–2 minutes. Reduce the heat and whisk in a little milk until combined and then continue whisking in the milk until it has all been absorbed. Add the bay leaf and simmer gently for 4–6 minutes until thickened, then season with salt and white pepper and grate in some nutmeg to taste.

Preheat the oven to 200°C/180°C fan/gas 6.

Remove the bay leaf from the bechamel and spread a little of the sauce in the bottom of a lasagne dish or deep ovenproof dish (about 20 x 30cm) then cover with sheets of lasagne (you are going to have 3 layers of pasta). Spread half the vegetable sauce over the sheets and top with a third of the remaining bechamel, lay more sheets of lasagne on top and cover with the remaining vegetable sauce. Spread with half of the remaining bechamel and arrange the remaining lasagne sheets on top. Finish with the remaining bechamel and spread to cover all of the pasta. Scatter over the cheese and drizzle with a little olive oil.

Bake in the oven for 50–60 minutes until golden and bubbling. Scatter with basil leaves and rest for 5 minutes before slicing.

Thai-Style Salad with Chilli-Pickled Cucumber

This is a wonderfully fresh and colourful vegan salad inspired by the bright flavours and contrasting textures of a Thai larb. I've used soya mince but, of course, use any mince you like – just adjust the cooking times accordingly.

SERVES 4

1 tbsp coconut oil
  or groundnut oil
1 banana shallot,
  thinly sliced
350g soya mince
3cm piece of fresh
  galangal or ginger,
  peeled and grated
2 garlic cloves, minced
1 lemongrass stalk,
  thinly sliced
2 tbsp low-sodium soy sauce
2 tsp sriracha
2 tsp palm or brown sugar
2 tsp Thai fish sauce (vegan)
zest and juice of 1 lime
a large handful of coriander,
  roughly chopped
a handful of mint leaves,
  roughly chopped
2 spring onions, trimmed
  and shredded
150g sugar snap peas,
  halved lengthways
150g edamame beans,
  cooked and refreshed
  under cold running water
1 carrot, peeled and cut into
  thin matchsticks or grated
1 red or yellow pepper, de-
  seeded and thinly sliced
1 romaine or 2 baby gem
  lettuce, thinly shredded
1 red chilli, de-seeded and
  finely sliced into rings
2 tsp sesame seeds, toasted

For the pickled cucumber
½ tsp chilli flakes
2–3 tbsp rice wine vinegar
  or white wine vinegar
1 tbsp brown sugar
a pinch of salt
½ cucumber, halved
  lengthways, de-seeded
  and sliced

First, make the pickled cucumber. Place all the ingredients for the pickle in a small bowl and whisk together until the sugar has dissolved. Add the cucumber and gently mix. Set aside while you make the salad.

Heat the oil in a deep-sided frying pan or wok and cook the shallot for 1–2 minutes until softened but not coloured. Add the soya mince and cook for 6–8 minutes or until it starts to brown. Add the galangal, garlic and lemongrass and cook for a further 1 minute. Stir in the soy, chilli sauce and the sugar and cook for a couple of minutes (don't worry if the pan seems dry). Add the fish sauce and a good squeeze of lime juice to taste. Remove from the heat and stir in half the coriander and mint and set aside to cool slightly.

In a large bowl, mix together the spring onions, sugar snap peas, edamame, carrot, pepper, lettuce, lime zest and chilli. Squeeze over a little lime juice and toss through the salad.

Spread the crunchy salad on a serving platter and arrange the mince on top. Finish with the remaining coriander, mint and the sesame seeds and serve with the pickled cucumber on top, or on the side as an accompaniment.

Spice-Roasted Cauliflower & Squash Traybake with Rice & Lentils

This is an easy and flavourful vegan-friendly traybake with mildly spiced roasted squash, and cauliflower and coconutty rice and lentils. I find a lot of traybakes are a little dry, so I love the way the coconut milk adds some creaminess as well as flavour. This is hassle-free cooking that's perfect for a busy day.

SERVES 4

1 medium cauliflower, broken into florets
1 small butternut squash, halved lengthways, de-seeded and cut into 1.5cm slices
1 red onion, peeled and cut into wedges
1 heaped tsp paprika (unsmoked)
½ tsp fennel seeds
½ tsp garlic powder (or 1 garlic clove, minced)
3–4 tbsp groundnut or light olive oil
1 x 400g tin lentils, drained and rinsed
1 x 250g pack microwave basmati rice
1 green chilli, de-seeded and chopped
2 tbsp chopped coriander, plus extra to serve
zest and juice of ½ lemon
1 x 400ml tin coconut milk
2 tsp mild or medium curry paste
a handful of cherry tomatoes cut in half
15g coconut flakes or flaked almonds
a pinch of Kashmiri red chilli flakes (optional)
sea salt and freshly ground black pepper

Preheat the oven to 200°C/180°C fan/gas 6.

Put the cauliflower, squash and onion in a large non-stick roasting tray and sprinkle with the paprika, the fennel seeds and garlic powder, and season with salt. Drizzle over the oil and gently toss to coat, ensuring everything is well coated. Arrange in a single layer (you may need two roasting tins). Roast for 20–25 minutes or until just tender and slightly caramelised around the edges.

In a bowl, toss the lentils and rice with a drizzle of oil, the chilli, coriander, lemon zest and a squeeze of the juice. Season well with salt and pepper. Stir the coconut milk in its tin to ensure the cream and water are combined then stir in the curry paste until well mixed. Remove the tray from the oven and turn the vegetables. Spoon the lentils and rice around the pumpkin and cauliflower and then pour the coconut milk over the rice, giving it a little stir here and there and making sure the veg aren't covered by the rice. Scatter over the tomatoes. Cook for another 12–15 minutes until the rice is warmed through and the vegetables are tender.

Meanwhile, toast the coconut flakes in a dry frying pan over a medium heat. Keep an eye on them because they can burn easily. Remove from the heat and set aside.

Remove the tray from the oven, squeeze over some lemon juice, scatter over the coconut flakes and some coriander and finish with a pinch of Kashmiri chilli flakes (if using).

Caraway & Orange Roasted Vegetables with Mixed Grains & Creamy Feta

You can buy pouches of pre-cooked mixed grains in supermarkets that are fantastic for making easy and healthy salads. I like using my Turkish-flavoured mix of bulgur wheat and couscous, but this tasty main-course salad also works well with barley or freekeh. I'm using summer veg but mix it up for the seasons – roasted roots are lovely for the autumn. I really like the creamy feta with the grains, although to save time you can crumble some feta on top if you prefer. Use a vegan feta-style cheese and plant-based yoghurt for a vegan version of this salad.

SERVES 4

1 large orange
1 large red onion, peeled and cut into 8 wedges
2 red peppers, de-seeded and cut into 1.5cm slices
1 aubergine, halved lengthways and cut into 1.5cm wedges
1 large courgette, cut on the diagonal into 1.5cm slices
4–5 garlic cloves, unpeeled
2–3 tbsp olive oil
2 tsp caraway seeds (or 1 tsp cumin seeds)
150g cherry tomatoes on the vine
35g walnut halves, roughly chopped, or almond slivers
1 tsp rose harissa paste
1 x 250g pouch ready-cooked mixed grains
1 tbsp chopped flat-leaf parsley, plus extra to serve
sea salt and freshly ground black pepper

For the creamy feta
100g feta, crumbled
100g Greek yoghurt
zest and juice of ½ lemon
1 tsp olive oil

Preheat the oven to 200°C/180°C fan/gas 6.

Place the crumbled feta, yoghurt and lemon zest in a small bowl and mix well with a fork. Mix in the olive oil, plus a little lemon juice to taste. Cover and chill until needed.

Cut the orange in half. Cut one half into thick slices, then cut all these slices in half again, to give quarter moons. Finely zest and juice the remaining half.

Put the onion, peppers, aubergine, courgette, garlic and orange slices into a large roasting tin or baking tray (you may need two trays). Drizzle over the oil and pour over half of the orange juice. Scatter over the caraway seeds, season with salt, toss well to coat and spread out in one layer. Roast for 25–30 minutes. Turn the vegetables and add the cherry tomatoes. Roast for a further 10–15 minutes until the vegetables are tender and slightly charred and the tomatoes have softened and started to blister.

Meanwhile, toast the walnuts in a dry frying pan over a medium heat for a couple of minutes. Keep an eye on them because they can burn easily. Stir in the harissa paste until the nuts are coated, then set aside.

Cook the grains according to the packet instructions and fluff with a fork. Remove the tray from the oven. Squeeze the garlic from their skins into the tray. Add the grains to the tray and stir through the remaining orange juice, the orange zest and the parsley. Check for seasoning.

Arrange the vegetables and grains on a serving platter. Scatter with parsley and the harissa walnuts and top with spoonfuls of the creamy feta. Serve with flatbreads or pitta.

Trofie Pasta with Pistachio & Mint Pesto

I first tried pistachio pesto on a filming visit to Sicily a good few years back and it quickly became a favourite of mine. Fresh and vibrant, it makes a lovely change from the usual pesto. It's also simple and quick to make and that's always a bonus! If you make any extra it's delicious on bruschetta or in sandwiches.

SERVES 4

45g shelled unsalted
  pistachio nuts
460g dried trofie pasta,
  or similar short pasta
1 small garlic clove,
  chopped
a pinch of chilli flakes
  (optional)
30g vegetarian Italian hard
  cheese (or Parmesan if
  non-vegetarian), grated,
  plus extra to serve
zest and juice of ½ lemon
15g mint leaves, shredded,
  plus extra to garnish
4–5 tbsp extra-virgin
  olive oil, plus extra
  for drizzling
sea salt and freshly
  ground black pepper

In a dry frying pan over a medium-high heat, toast the pistachios for a minute or two until lightly golden. Keep an eye on them because they can easily burn. Remove from the heat and set aside.

Cook the pasta in a large saucepan of well salted boiling water according to the packet instructions, until al dente. Drain the pasta, reserving some of the cooking liquid.

Meanwhile, put the garlic, a pinch each of salt and pepper, the pistachios, chilli flakes (if using), grated cheese, lemon zest and mint in a food processor and pulse until coarsely ground. Add a squeeze of lemon juice and 2 tablespoons of the oil and pulse a couple of times to combine. Drizzle in a little more oil as you pulse until you reach the desired consistency – you're looking for a thick wet pesto with a coarse texture. Alternatively, pound the ingredients in a pestle and mortar and stir in the oil. Check the seasoning and add more lemon juice if needed. Set aside.

Put the pasta back into the pan and stir in the pesto, 2 tablespoons of the reserved pasta cooking water and a good squeeze of lemon juice. Stir to combine over a very low heat, adding another tablespoon of pasta water if needed to form a glossy sauce. Check for seasoning.

Serve in warmed pasta bowls, drizzled with a little extra-virgin olive oil, scattered with cheese and garnished with mint leaves.

Tikka Paneer with Coriander & Mint Chutney

Paneer is a non-melting Indian cheese that's great for taking on flavours and cooking over a high heat, so these juicy paneer kebabs bursting with punchy Indian spices are perfect for a summer barbecue. You can make them vegan by swapping the paneer for tofu and using dairy-free yoghurt. Serve with my chickpea salad (page 215) and coriander flatbreads (page 170).

MAKES 8 SKEWERS

1 tbsp gram (chickpea) flour
1 tbsp oil, plus extra
  for drizzling
2 tbsp tikka masala paste
1 heaped tsp Kashmiri
  chilli powder
¼ tsp ground turmeric
2 garlic cloves, minced
3cm piece of fresh root
  ginger, peeled and grated
180g Greek yoghurt
½ lemon, for squeezing
1 red onion, peeled and
  cut into 3cm chunks
1 x 500g block paneer,
  cut into 3cm pieces
2 red peppers, de-seeded
  and cut into 3cm chunks
1 tsp chaat masala (optional)
sea salt

*For the coriander
  and mint chutney*
a bunch of coriander, leaves
  picked (about 20g)
a handful of mint leaves
1–2 green chillies,
  de-seeded and chopped
2cm piece of fresh root
  ginger, peeled
  and chopped
1 tbsp lemon juice
1 tsp sugar
a good pinch of salt
2 tbsp Greek yoghurt

In a dry frying pan over a medium heat, toast the gram flour until lightly toasted and golden. Set aside to cool.

In a bowl, whisk together the oil, tikka masala paste, chilli powder, turmeric, garlic, ginger, cooled gram flour and ½ teaspoon salt. Add the yoghurt and a good squeeze of lemon juice and mix well to form a wet paste consistency.

Separate the red onion chunks into individual leaves. Add the paneer, peppers and onion pieces to the paste and toss to coat. Leave to marinate for at least 30 minutes, or longer if you have the time.

To make the chutney, put the coriander and mint in a food processor with 1 tablespoon of water and blitz until well chopped. Add the chillies, ginger, lemon juice, sugar, salt and yoghurt and pulse until you get a green sauce. Put into a small bowl and chill until needed.

Preheat the oven to 220°C/200°C fan/gas 7 (or preheat the barbecue to medium-high).

Skewer the paneer, peppers and onions onto 8 skewers, alternating as you go. Drizzle or spray the skewers with a little oil and place on a wire rack above a baking tray. Bake in the hot oven for 12–15 minutes or until golden, turning once. You can char further under a hot grill if you like. If cooking on the barbecue or in a chargrill pan, cook on a lightly oiled grill/griddle for 8–10 minutes, turning and basting occasionally.

Serve the kebabs sprinkled with chaat masala (if using), alongside the chickpea salad, chutney and some flatbreads.

Broccoli & Cauliflower Gratin with Grated Halloumi & Dukkah

This veggie gratin is a lighter alternative to cauliflower cheese and makes a delightful veggie lunch. It's full of flavour and texture from the crispy and gently spiced dukkah topping. Dukkah, a traditional Egyptian spice blend, is readily available from most supermarkets or you can make your own with a blend of toasted and blitzed nuts, sesame seeds, sumac, coriander and cumin seeds.

SERVES 4

1 small cauliflower (about 650g), broken into florets
olive oil, for drizzling
1 garlic clove, minced
1 head of broccoli (about 350g), broken into florets
300g crème fraîche
zest and juice of ½ lemon
1 tsp Dijon mustard
150g halloumi, grated
2 tbsp fresh breadcrumbs
1 tbsp chopped flat-leaf parsley
2 tbsp dukkah
sea salt and freshly ground black pepper

Preheat the oven to 200°C/180°C fan/gas 6.

Put the cauliflower florets in a gratin or baking dish and drizzle with oil. Scatter over the garlic, season with salt and pepper and toss to coat. Roast for 10 minutes. Add the broccoli to the dish, drizzle with a little more oil and roast for a further 10 minutes.

In a bowl, mix together the crème fraîche, lemon zest and juice, and mustard, and season to taste. Spoon over the roasted vegetables and toss to coat. Scatter the halloumi evenly over the top. Mix together the breadcrumbs, parsley and dukkah and scatter on top. Bake for a further 20–25 minutes or until golden and crisp.

Mushroom Beanballs in Tomato Sauce

Simple, comforting and tasty – meatballs are a firm family favourite for a hearty meal, and my homemade vegan beanballs are just as satisfying. They're full of flavour and texture and are sure to please everyone. Delicious served with spaghetti, rice or couscous for an easy meat-free dinner.

SERVES 4

1 tbsp olive oil, plus extra
    for greasing and drizzling
½ red onion, finely chopped
150g button mushrooms,
    roughly chopped
1 tsp Italian dried
    mixed herbs
2 garlic cloves, minced
1 x 400g tin mixed pulses
    in water or kidney beans,
    drained, rinsed and
    patted dry
60g jumbo rolled oats
1 tbsp tomato purée
½ tsp sea salt
½ tsp ground black pepper
1 tbsp pine nuts, lightly
    bashed

For the tomato sauce
2 tbsp extra-virgin olive oil
½ red onion, finely chopped
2 garlic cloves, minced
1 medium-hot red chilli,
    de-seeded and finely
    chopped (optional)
500g passata
150ml vegetable stock
½ tsp sugar
½ tbsp balsamic vinegar
8–10 basil leaves, shredded,
    plus extra to serve
sea salt and freshly
    ground black pepper

Preheat the oven to 200°C/180°C fan/gas 6. Lightly oil a non-stick baking tray.

Heat the oil in a non-stick frying pan over a medium heat and add the onion and mushrooms. Cook for 4–6 minutes until softened. Add the herbs and garlic and cook for another 30 seconds. Set aside to cool.

Put the pulses, oats and tomato purée in a food processor and blitz until well combined. Add the onion mixture, salt and pepper and blitz again. (I like to leave plenty of texture but feel free to blitz for longer if you prefer.) Add the pine nuts and pulse a couple of times to combine. With slightly damp hands, form the mixture into golf-ball- or walnut-sized balls (you should get 12–16 balls, depending on size). Place the beanballs on the oiled baking tray and drizzle with a little more oil. Bake in the oven for 18–20 minutes, turning once.

Meanwhile, make the tomato sauce. Heat the oil in a sauté or deep-sided frying pan over a medium heat. Add the onion and cook for 4–6 minutes until softened but not coloured. Add the garlic and chilli (if using) and cook for 30 seconds until fragrant.

Add the passata, stock and sugar. Season with salt and black pepper, stir and bring to the boil. Reduce the heat and simmer gently for 10 minutes. Stir in the balsamic vinegar and basil.

Remove the beanballs from the oven and drop them gently into the tomato sauce. Simmer over a low heat for 3–4 minutes, turning once in the sauce. Scatter with basil and serve with spaghetti, rice or couscous.

Honey & Thyme Caramelised Pear, Pecan & Cheese Tart

This easy-to-make sweet and savoury tart is gorgeous, with flavours that make me very happy indeed. Creamy, tangy goat's cheese with buttery pear and aromatic thyme and the warm honey bringing sweetness – it's just delightful! I've used a little blue cheese to add a burst of contrasting sharpness, but if you prefer you can leave it out and use a little more goat's cheese. Serve with a watercress or rocket salad.

SERVES 4

25g butter
2 tbsp runny honey
2 firm pears, cored
   and sliced
½ lemon, for squeezing
1 x 500g block ready-made
   puff pastry
plain flour, for dusting
125g soft goat's cheese
100g dolcelatte or similar
   soft blue cheese
a handful of pecans or
   walnuts, roughly chopped
leaves of 3–4 thyme sprigs
   (or whole sprigs if soft)
1 egg, beaten
   (or a little milk)
sea salt and freshly
   ground black pepper

Preheat the oven to 200°C/180°C fan/gas 6. Line a baking sheet with baking parchment.

In a large frying pan over a medium heat, melt the butter with the honey. Add the pears and a squeeze of lemon juice and cook for 2 minutes on each side until caramelised. Remove the pears from the pan and lightly season, reserving the honey caramel in the pan.

Roll out the pastry on a lightly floured work surface to a rectangle about 28 x 38cm and 5mm thick. Score a 2cm border around the edge of the pastry then place it on the lined baking sheet.

Arrange the pear slices over the pastry within the border, then dot the cheeses over in an even layer, then the pecans. Scatter over the thyme. Lightly brush the border with the beaten egg.

Bake for 15–20 minutes until the pastry is puffed and golden and the cheese is bubbling. Season and drizzle with a little of the leftover caramel to serve, either warm or cold.

Mac 'n' Cheese with Chard & Leeks

You really can't beat a good mac 'n' cheese – it's simple home cooking at its best and the perfect comfort food. I've jazzed up a classic recipe with some chard and leeks and a crunchy herby top for this delicious family supper or indulgent side dish. You can use spinach or young kale in place of chard if you prefer.

SERVES 4–6

40g butter, plus extra
  for greasing
1 tbsp olive oil
1 medium leek, trimmed
  and finely sliced
1 garlic clove, minced
150g Swiss or rainbow
  chard, stems and ribs
  removed, chopped
1 tbsp water
300g dried macaroni
40g plain flour
1 tsp English mustard
700ml full-fat milk
200g vegetarian mature
  Cheddar, grated
sea salt and ground
  white pepper

For the herby top
40g coarse fresh
  breadcrumbs
30g vegetarian Italian hard
  cheese (or Parmesan
  if non-vegetarian),
  finely grated
1 tbsp finely chopped
  flat-leaf parsley,
  plus extra to serve
a pinch of cayenne pepper
  (optional)
a drizzle of olive oil

Preheat the oven to 200°C/180°C fan/gas 6. Grease a large (about 26 x 18 x 5cm) ovenproof dish with butter.

Heat the oil in a frying pan over a medium heat and cook the leek for 3–4 minutes until softened and just beginning to brown. Add the garlic and cook for 30 seconds until fragrant. Stir in the chopped chard leaves and water. Sauté for 2–3 minutes until wilted and any liquid has evaporated. Season with salt and pepper and set aside.

Bring a large pan of salted water to the boil and stir in the macaroni. Cook for 2 minutes less than the packet instructions, until just al dente – don't overcook because it will cook further in the oven. Drain and return to the pan.

Meanwhile, melt the butter in a saucepan over a low heat. When foaming, stir in the flour and cook for 1 minute, stirring constantly. Add the mustard and, over a very low heat, gradually whisk in the milk. Turn up the heat a little, stirring constantly, until you have a steady simmer, and continue to cook and whisk until you have a nicely thickened sauce. Take off the heat and add the grated Cheddar, stirring until melted. Season with plenty of white pepper and a little salt.

Stir the chard and leeks through the macaroni until well distributed, then add the cheese sauce. Mix to combine, check for seasoning and then pour into the baking dish.

Combine the breadcrumbs with the grated cheese, parsley, cayenne (if using) and a little drizzle of oil. Scatter over the top of the macaroni. Bake for 15–20 minutes, or until golden-brown and bubbling. Serve immediately, garnished with more parsley.

One-Pot Asparagus & Artichoke Orzo with Spinach & Pine Nuts

A one-pot dish is a splendid thing – minimum effort and minimal mess are just what we need after a hectic day. This is fresh with the summery flavours of asparagus and lemon, and velvety and indulgent with orzo, salty cheese and buttery artichokes. Delicious! For a change you can swap the hard cheese for feta.

SERVES 4

2 tbsp extra-virgin olive oil,
    plus extra for drizzling
2 garlic cloves,
    finely chopped
¼ tsp chilli flakes
zest and juice of 1 lemon
250g asparagus spears,
    trimmed and halved
1 banana shallot,
    finely chopped
300g dried orzo pasta
600ml vegetable stock
240g artichoke hearts in
    water or oil, drained
    and quartered
3 tbsp pine nuts
75g vegetarian Italian hard
    cheese (or Parmesan if
    non-vegetarian), grated
80g baby spinach leaves,
    chopped
a handful of basil leaves,
    chopped
sea salt and freshly
    ground black pepper

Preheat the oven to 200°C/180°C fan/gas 6.

In a bowl, mix together 1 tablespoon of the olive oil, half the garlic, the chilli flakes, half the lemon zest and a squeeze of juice. Add the asparagus, season well with salt and pepper and toss to coat.

Add the remaining tablespoon of oil to a wide flameproof casserole over a medium heat. Add the shallot and cook for 1–2 minutes until softened. Add the remaining garlic and cook for 30 seconds until fragrant, then stir in the orzo and toast for 1–2 minutes. Pour in the stock, season with pepper, stir and bring to the boil. Remove from the heat, stir in the artichokes and the remaining lemon zest. Place the asparagus on top of the orzo, drizzling over any of the marinade. Transfer to the oven and cook, uncovered, for 18–20 minutes until the orzo is tender but still with bite.

Meanwhile, in a small, dry frying pan over a medium heat, toast the pine nuts for 1–2 minutes until golden. Keep an eye on them because they can easily burn. Tip onto a plate.

Remove the orzo from the oven. Lift out a few of the roasted asparagus spears from the top to reserve for garnish and immediately stir through half the grated cheese, the chopped spinach, basil, a drizzle of extra-virgin olive oil and plenty of lemon juice to taste. Check for seasoning, cover and leave to rest for a minute or two. Serve topped with the reserved asparagus, toasted pine nuts and remaining cheese.

Jackfruit, Butter Bean & Okra Pimento Pot

This vibrant vegan dish is delicately flavoured with the distinctive spice of pimento berries (allspice). It's proper food for the soul, packed full of goodness, and is as colourful as it is delicious. Jackfruit is becoming increasingly popular for vegan dishes – its fibrous texture is excellent at taking on flavours. This is a comforting stew the whole family can enjoy – just take it easy with the Scotch bonnet or keep it whole and remove before serving.

SERVES 4–6

2 tbsp coconut oil
   or sunflower oil
1 large onion, chopped
½–1 Scotch bonnet chilli,
   de-seeded and chopped
3 garlic cloves, minced
5cm piece of fresh root
   ginger, peeled and grated
8–10 whole allspice
   (pimento) berries
1 cinnamon stick
2 tsp fresh thyme leaves
¼ tsp ground turmeric
a large handful of coriander,
   leaves and stalks
   separated, chopped
1 x 560g tin young jackfruit,
   drained, rinsed and
   cut into chunks
2 peppers (red and/or
   yellow), de-seeded and
   cut into 2.5cm chunks
2 sweet potatoes (about
   250g in total), peeled and
   cut into 2.5cm chunks
1 x 400g tin butter beans,
   drained and rinsed
2 large tomatoes,
   roughly chopped
300–350ml vegetable stock
2 tsp dark muscovado sugar
1 x 400ml tin coconut milk
100g fresh or frozen okra,
   trimmed and cut into
   2cm slices
juice of 1 lime
a small bag (about 60g)
   of baby spinach leaves
sea salt and freshly
   ground black pepper

In a large, heavy-based saucepan or flameproof casserole, melt the coconut oil over a medium heat. Add the onion and cook for 4–6 minutes until soft but not coloured, then add the chilli, garlic, ginger, allspice, cinnamon, thyme, turmeric and coriander stalks. Continue to cook for a minute, until fragrant. Stir in the jackfruit and cook in the spices for another couple of minutes.

Add the peppers, sweet potatoes, beans and tomatoes, stir until coated in all the spices, then add 300ml of the stock, and the sugar. Bring to the boil then reduce the heat, cover and simmer for 10–15 minutes, stirring occasionally and adding more stock if needed. Add the coconut milk, okra, half the coriander leaves and a good squeeze of lime juice. Season to taste and simmer over a low-medium heat, uncovered, for another 15–20 minutes or until everything is tender. Stir in the spinach until just wilted.

Check for seasoning and add more lime juice to taste. Ladle into warm bowls, sprinkle with plenty of chopped coriander leaves and serve.

Island Black Bean Burgers with Avocado Salsa

These vegan black bean burgers are full of texture and Caribbean spice. The crunchy peanut butter and bite of the cashew nuts adds a nice bit of body, and the polenta gives a good crisp coating. I love them spicy, but you can leave the chilli out if you prefer. If you have a nut allergy, try using tahini in place of the peanut butter, and stir in some sunflower seeds instead of the cashews.

SERVES 4

2 tbsp sunflower or coconut oil, plus extra for drizzling
½ red onion, finely chopped
1 small red pepper, de-seeded and finely diced
1 small garlic clove, minced
1 medium-hot red chilli, de-seeded and finely chopped
1 tbsp jerk seasoning
45g cashew nuts
1 x 400g tin black beans, drained, rinsed and patted dry
125g ready-to-eat brown rice or bulgur wheat
1 heaped tbsp crunchy peanut butter
1 tbsp vegan mayo
25g panko breadcrumbs
a handful of coriander leaves
zest of ½ lime
3 tbsp fine polenta
sea salt and freshly ground black pepper

For the salsa
1 large avocado, peeled, stoned and finely diced
2 ripe vine tomatoes, de-seeded and finely chopped
½ red onion, finely chopped
2 tbsp chopped coriander
a pinch of caster sugar
zest and juice of ½ lime

For the hot pepper mayo
3–4 tbsp vegan mayo
hot pepper sauce, to taste

To serve
4 burger buns, halved
crisp lettuce leaves, shredded

Heat a drizzle of oil in a frying pan, add the onion and pepper and gently sweat over a low-medium heat for 3–4 minutes until a little softened. Add the garlic, chilli and jerk seasoning and cook for another 30 seconds until fragrant. Set aside to cool.

Pulse the nuts in a food processor until coarsely chopped, then tip into a large bowl. Put the softened onion and pepper, half the black beans, the rice, peanut butter, mayo, breadcrumbs, coriander and lime zest into the food processor. Season well and blitz for 30–45 seconds until well combined. Scrape the mixture from the sides and blitz again until combined but still with plenty of texture. Transfer to the bowl with the nuts and remaining beans and mix well with your hands, adding a little more peanut butter or mayonnaise if the mixture is too dry, or breadcrumbs if too wet. Divide the mixture evenly into 4 and shape into burger patties with your hands. Cover and chill for 30 minutes to firm up.

Meanwhile, mix the salsa ingredients together in a bowl to combine. Season with salt to taste and set aside.

In a small bowl, mix together the hot pepper mayo ingredients.

Spread the polenta on a plate with a small pinch of salt and gently coat the patties on all sides.

Heat a frying pan over a medium-high heat and add the oil. When hot, add the burgers, reduce the heat to medium and cook for 3–4 minutes without moving. Gently turn over and cook on the other side for 3–4 minutes or until heated through and a crust has formed. (Alternatively, spray the burgers with oil and bake in the oven at 200°C/180°C fan/gas 6 for 12–15 minutes or until crispy.)

Lightly char or toast the burger buns, then spread a dollop of the hot pepper mayo onto the base. Add some shredded lettuce, top with a burger and add a good spoonful of salsa. Top with a little more hot pepper mayo and finish with the burger bun top.

Pizza Margherita

A family favourite and something I love to make for my grown-up kids when they're at home. A margherita pizza is a great vehicle for your favourite toppings (I love chargrilled artichokes and black olives) so feel free to add extras if you like – although not too much because you're likely to end up with a soggy bottom! You can now buy vegan mozzarella that melts well if you want a vegan-friendly pizza.

MAKES 2 LARGE PIZZAS

300g strong white bread flour, plus extra for dusting
1 tsp fast-action dried yeast
1 tsp salt
2 tbsp extra-virgin olive oil, plus extra for greasing and drizzling
200ml warm water
150–200ml crushed tomatoes or passata
1 small garlic clove, minced
a pinch of chilli flakes (optional)
4–6 basil leaves, chopped, plus extra to serve
2 tsp semolina or fine polenta
20g vegetarian Italian hard cheese (or Parmesan if non-vegetarian), grated
1 x 125g ball of mozzarella, patted dry and torn or sliced
sea salt and freshly ground black pepper
chilli oil, to serve (optional)

Place the flour, yeast and salt in a bowl. Mix the oil and warm water in a jug. Slowly pour the liquid into the dry ingredients, mixing with a wooden spoon until everything comes together. The dough will be fairly wet at this point. Tip out onto a lightly floured work surface and then knead for 4–5 minutes with lightly floured hands until you have a soft, stretchy dough. Transfer the dough to a lightly oiled bowl, rub the top with a little oil, then cover with a clean, slightly damp tea towel. Set aside at room temperature for 1–1½ hours or until the dough has doubled in size.

Meanwhile, mix the crushed tomatoes with the garlic, chilli flakes (if using) and basil. Season to taste and set aside.

Preheat the oven to 220°C/200°C fan/gas 7 and place 1 or 2 large baking sheets or a pizza stone in the oven to heat up.

Knock the air out of the dough. Knead for a minute until smooth, then cut in half and shape into two balls. Let rest for 10 minutes, then roll each out on a floured work surface to a 20–25cm round.

Sprinkle the semolina onto 2 sheets of baking parchment and place the pizza bases on top. Use your hands to stretch the dough out further – particularly if you prefer a thinner base – and use your fingers to indent a slightly raised rim for the crust.

Spread a thin layer of the tomato sauce over the bases, using the back of a spoon and avoiding the rim.

Scatter evenly with the hard cheese and then the mozzarella. Drizzle with a little extra-virgin olive oil and carefully slide the pizzas with the baking parchment onto your hot tray (remove the paper if using a stone or a very hot pizza oven) and bake for 14–16 minutes (it may be easier to cook one at a time) until the base is crisp and the cheeses are bubbling and lightly golden.

Garnish with fresh basil leaves and drizzle with a little chilli oil (if using) or extra-virgin olive oil. Serve immediately.

Spicy Three Bean & Pepper Chilli Pot

You can't beat a tasty bowl of hot chilli for an easy and comforting one-pot, and mine is full of flavour and spice; you don't have to be vegan to love this dish. Adjust the chilli content to suit your taste – I like it quite fiery and topped with cooling yoghurt and avocado. Perfect served at the table in its pot with crunchy tortilla chips for dipping. Don't forget the ice-cold beers!

SERVES 4–6

2 tbsp coconut or olive oil
1 large red onion, finely chopped
2 peppers (red and yellow) de-seeded and cut into chunks
1 celery stick, trimmed and finely chopped
4 garlic cloves, minced
1 medium-hot red chilli, de-seeded and finely chopped
2 tsp ground cumin
½–1 tsp hot chilli powder or cayenne, to taste
1 tsp sweet smoked paprika
½ tsp ground allspice
a large handful of coriander, stalks and leaves separated, chopped, plus extra leaves to serve
1 tsp dried oregano
450–500ml vegetable stock, hot
1 × 400g tin chopped tomatoes
1 tbsp tomato purée
1 tbsp maple syrup
3 x 400g tins beans (kidney, pinto and cannellini), drained and rinsed
1 small cinnamon stick
1 lime, for squeezing
25g dark chocolate (70% cocoa), chopped
sea salt

To serve
plant-based thick plain yoghurt or soured cream
chopped avocado
tortilla chips

Heat the oil in a large, heavy-based saucepan or flameproof casserole over a medium heat and add the onion, peppers and celery. Cook for 4–6 minutes, stirring often, until softened. Add the garlic and chilli and stir for 30 seconds, then stir in the ground spices, coriander stalks and oregano and cook for 1–2 minutes, adding a splash of stock if needed.

Add the chopped tomatoes, tomato purée and maple syrup and give everything a good stir, scraping the bottom of the pan. Add the beans, cinnamon and 450ml of the stock and season with salt. Bring to the boil, cover with a lid, reduce the heat and simmer for 10 minutes.

Remove the lid and gently simmer, uncovered, for another 20–25 minutes, until thickened, stirring occasionally and adding a splash more stock to loosen if needed. Stir in the coriander leaves, squeeze in some lime juice to taste and check the seasoning. Stir in the chocolate, allowing it to melt.

Serve at the table for everyone to tuck in. Spoon into warm bowls, top with a spoonful of yoghurt and chopped avocado and scatter with coriander leaves. Serve with tortilla chips.

Chapter Three
FISH & SEAFOOD

Mediterranean Salmon Burgers & Potato Salad

Simple and delicious, these salmon burgers are great for an easy light lunch or to serve at a barbecue. The Greek flavours in the potato salad and the cucumber yoghurt are the perfect summery accompaniments to add some Mediterranean flavour to your al fresco dining.

SERVES 4

4 skinless, boneless salmon
  fillets (600g in total),
  from a sustainable source
2 tsp Dijon mustard
zest and juice of 1 lemon
1 tbsp Greek yoghurt
1 tsp finely chopped fresh
  oregano or ½ tsp dried
1 tbsp finely chopped
  flat-leaf parsley
¼ tsp salt
¼ tsp chilli flakes (optional)
oil, for drizzling

For the potato salad
750g waxy potatoes,
  scrubbed
zest and juice of 1 lemon
4 tbsp extra-virgin olive oil,
  plus extra if needed
1 small garlic clove, minced
½ red onion, thinly sliced
1 tsp fresh oregano leaves
  or ½ tsp dried
a handful of flat-leaf
  parsley, chopped
60g black olives,
  pitted and halved
sea salt and freshly
  ground black pepper

For the cucumber yoghurt
¼ cucumber, grated
5 tbsp Greek yoghurt
1 small garlic clove, minced
1 tsp lemon juice
1 tbsp chopped mint leaves

To serve
pitta pockets or folded
  flatbreads
a handful of rocket leaves
sliced vine tomatoes

First, make the cucumber mint yoghurt. Squeeze any excess water from the grated cucumber then add to a bowl with the remaining ingredients. Season with salt and pepper and mix well. Chill until needed.

Pat the salmon dry and, using a sharp knife, finely dice three quarters of it. Place in a large bowl. Add the remaining salmon to a food processor with the mustard, lemon zest and 1 teaspoon of lemon juice. Blend to a smooth paste. Tip into the bowl with the diced salmon and add the yoghurt, herbs, salt and chilli flakes (if using). Mix until well combined.

Using slightly damp hands, squeeze and shape the salmon into 4 burgers or 8 small burgers and chill for 20 minutes to firm up.

Meanwhile, make the potato salad. Add the potatoes to a large saucepan of cold salted water and bring to the boil. Cook for 15–20 minutes depending on size, or until tender and easily pierced with a blunt knife. Drain, and while hot, cut in half or into chunks and place in a bowl. Mix the lemon juice with the olive oil and garlic and add to the warm potatoes, mixing well to combine. Add the zest, onion and oregano and stir well. Season and set aside.

Preheat the barbecue to medium or heat a non-stick frying pan over a medium heat and drizzle in a little oil. Cook the salmon burgers for 2–3 minutes on each side or until lightly golden and cooked through.

Toss the parsley and olives through the potato salad, check for seasoning and add a touch more extra-virgin olive oil if needed.

Fill the pittas with rocket leaves, tomato slices and the salmon burgers, topped with cucumber mint yoghurt, and serve the potato salad on the side.

Harissa-Crusted Cod with Quick Chickpea, Spinach & Tomato Stew

Having a jar of harissa in your cupboard or fridge really helps when you need something to add some spice and punch to your cooking, and this is a speedy and flavoursome meal that's perfect for mid-week. Here the harissa adds an aromatic smokiness to the delicate fish. Serve with a side of couscous or slices of fresh bread, if you like.

SERVES 4

1 tsp caraway seeds
2 tbsp olive oil, plus
    extra for greasing
a pinch of ground cumin
2 garlic cloves, minced
1 heaped tsp tomato purée
2 x 400g tin chickpeas,
    drained and rinsed
1 x 400g tin chopped
    tomatoes
a handful of cherry
    tomatoes, halved
    (optional)
175ml vegetable stock
a good pinch of sugar
150g baby spinach leaves
zest and juice of ½ lemon
2 tbsp finely chopped
    flat-leaf parsley,
    plus extra to garnish
80g fresh breadcrumbs
1½–2 tbsp harissa paste
4 x 140g skinless and
    boneless thick-cut cod
    (or similar white fish)
    fillets or loins, from
    a sustainable source
sea salt and freshly
    ground black pepper

Preheat the oven to 200°C/180°C fan/gas 6.

Put the caraway seeds in a deep-sided frying pan that has a lid over a medium heat and toast for 30 seconds until fragrant. Add 1 tablespoon of the oil then the cumin and garlic and cook for a further 30 seconds until fragrant. Stir in the tomato purée and chickpeas until well coated then add the tinned tomatoes, cherry tomatoes (if using), 150ml of the stock and the sugar. Season well with salt and pepper. Bring to the boil, reduce the heat, cover and simmer for 5–6 minutes, stirring occasionally.

Remove the lid and simmer for another 6–8 minutes, adding a splash more stock if needed. Stir in the spinach a handful at a time until just wilted. Give a good squeeze of lemon juice, check for seasoning and stir in 1 tablespoon of the parsley.

Meanwhile, in a small bowl, mix together the breadcrumbs, harissa paste, lemon zest, and the remaining parsley and olive oil. Season the fish fillets and place on a lightly oiled baking tray. Spread the harissa breadcrumbs over the top of each fillet, lightly pressing them down to stick. Bake in the oven for 10–14 minutes depending on the thickness of your fillets, or until the top is crispy and the fish is cooked through (it should be opaque and flake easily).

Spoon the chickpeas into shallow serving bowls and place a cod fillet on top. Scatter with parsley and serve immediately.

Pan-Fried Hake with Brown Butter, Cauliflower Purée & Spring Greens

You only need a few simple ingredients for this delicious fish dish and the result is an elegant yet indulgent plate of food – perfect for a special dinner for two. When not in season, swap the spring greens for some cabbage or kale.

SERVES 2

200g spring greens, thick
   stalks removed, shredded
extra-virgin olive oil,
   for drizzling
zest and juice of ½ lemon
2 x 150g hake, halibut or
   cod fillets, skin-on, from
   a sustainable source
75g butter
2 tsp capers (optional)
1 tbsp finely chopped
   flat-leaf parsley
salt and ground
   white pepper

For the cauliflower purée
1 tbsp light olive oil, plus
   extra for drizzling
1 shallot, chopped
1 small garlic clove,
   chopped
1 small cauliflower
   (about 400g), broken
   into small florets
100ml double cream or milk
400ml vegetable stock

First, make the cauliflower purée. Heat the oil in a saucepan over a medium heat, add the shallot and cook for 1–2 minutes until softened but not coloured. Add the garlic and cook for 30 seconds until fragrant, then add the cauliflower and cook for 2–3 minutes, stirring. Add the cream and stock and bring to a simmer. Cook for 10–12 minutes until the cauliflower is tender. Use a slotted spoon to transfer the cauliflower to a blender, and pulse. Add enough of the cooking liquid to blend to a smooth purée. Season with salt and white pepper and keep warm.

Meanwhile, bring a large saucepan of salted water to the boil and add the spring greens. Cook for 3–4 minutes or until tender. Drain well, drizzle with extra-virgin olive oil and stir in the lemon zest. Season with salt and white pepper and add lemon juice to taste.

Heat a large non-stick frying pan over a medium heat. Drizzle the hake fillets with light olive oil, season with salt and place in the pan, skin-side down. Leave for 3–4 minutes until the skin has become crisp, then gently turn over. Add 1 tablespoon of the butter to the pan and cook for 2–3 minutes, depending on the thickness of your fillets, basting with the butter as it cooks, until the fish is cooked through. Remove the fish from the pan and keep warm. Add the remaining butter to the pan and increase the heat to medium-high. Cook for 2–3 minutes, stirring frequently until golden-brown – keep an eye on it because you don't want it to burn. Remove from the heat and add a squeeze of lemon. Stir in the capers (if using) and parsley.

To serve, spoon some cauliflower purée onto plates and top with the fish, with the spring greens to the side. Spoon the brown butter over the fish.

Crab & Lemon Linguine with Pangrattato

This is a quick and easy pasta dish that's so summery and light. Crab has a lovely delicate flavour that works well with lemon and a hint of chilli. Fresh crab meat is best, but you can use a packet or even tinned for this recipe if you can't get hold of any. The zesty breadcrumb topping adds a lovely crispy texture. When you fancy a change you can swap the crab for a tin of good-quality tuna.

SERVES 2

200g dried linguine pasta
3 tbsp extra-virgin olive oil, plus extra for drizzling
2 garlic cloves, finely chopped
1 medium-hot red chilli, de-seeded and finely chopped
30ml dry white wine (optional)
zest and juice of 1 lemon
150g cooked white crab meat
1 tbsp chopped flat-leaf parsley
sea salt and freshly ground black pepper

For the breadcrumb topping
1 thick slice of day-old bread
zest of ½ lemon
2 tsp olive oil
1 tbsp chopped flat-leaf parsley

Preheat the oven to 200°C/180°C fan/gas 6.

First, make the breadcrumb topping. Pulse the slice of bread with the lemon zest in a mini food processor until you have coarse breadcrumbs. Add the olive oil and parsley and pulse once or twice until combined. Season with salt and pepper. Spread out on a baking tray and bake for 7–10 minutes until golden brown and crispy. Remove from the oven and set aside.

Meanwhile, cook the pasta in a large saucepan of salted boiling water according to the packet instructions, until al dente. Drain, reserving a little of the cooking water, and drizzle with olive oil to prevent it sticking.

In a deep-sided frying pan over a low heat, add the extra-virgin olive oil, garlic and chilli and cook for 1 minute until fragrant and starting to sizzle but not brown. Turn up the heat to medium and add the wine (if using) and a squeeze of lemon juice. Allow to bubble for 1 minute then reduce the heat back to low-medium. Stir in the crab meat, 2 tablespoons of the reserved pasta water, the lemon zest and another good squeeze of juice, and season with salt and pepper to taste. Cook gently for a minute until the crab is warmed through. Tip in the pasta and toss over the gentle heat until well coated in the sauce, adding a little more reserved pasta water if needed. Stir through the parsley and check for seasoning. Serve immediately, drizzled with extra-virgin olive oil and topped with the crispy breadcrumbs.

Smoked Salmon Super Salad with Dill & Turmeric Dressing

This salad is loaded with good-for-you ingredients, and it makes a satisfying main course. You don't need too much smoked salmon, so you can buy the small packets of slices available in supermarkets. Dill is a delicate aromatic herb that works perfectly with the salmon, and the addition of a little turmeric in the dressing adds a subtle warmth. The salad is just as delightful with smoked mackerel fillets.

SERVES 4

150g young kale leaves, stems removed, leaves shredded (or use mixed salad leaves)
1 lemon, for squeezing
extra-virgin olive oil, for drizzling
2 spring onions, trimmed and finely sliced
1 green apple, cored, quartered and thinly sliced
1 small fennel bulb, cored and thinly sliced, fronds reserved for garnish
200g pre-cooked quinoa
180g smoked salmon slices, from a sustainable source, cut into strips
1 large ripe avocado, peeled, stoned and sliced
1 medium-hot red chilli, de-seeded and finely sliced into rings (optional)
2 tbsp seeds (sunflower and/or pumpkin)
1 tbsp roughly chopped dill
sea salt and freshly ground black pepper
lemon wedges, to serve

For the dill and turmeric dressing
120ml low-fat plain yoghurt
2 tsp extra-virgin olive oil
1–2 tsp runny honey
1 tbsp finely chopped dill
¼–½ tsp ground turmeric
½ lemon, for squeezing

First, make the dressing. In a small bowl, whisk together the yoghurt, oil, 1 teaspoon honey, dill and ¼ teaspoon turmeric. Add lemon juice to taste. Season with salt and adjust the turmeric and honey according to taste. Set aside.

Put the kale (or salad leaves) in a large bowl, squeeze over some lemon juice and drizzle with a little oil. Toss to coat and, if using kale, massage with your hands for a minute to soften the leaves.

Add the spring onion, apple and fennel and swirl gently to coat. Toss through the cooked quinoa, drizzle with a little more oil and lemon juice, and season with salt to taste.

Tip the salad onto a serving plate and arrange the salmon and avocado slices on top. Sprinkle over the chilli, seeds, dill and fennel fronds, drizzle with the dressing and season with a good grind of black pepper. Serve with fresh bread and lemon wedges for squeezing.

Speedy Sautéed Salmon in Cherry Tomato & Basil Sauce

Salmon is great for taking on flavours, and with just a few ingredients it's easy to have an inviting meal ready in under half an hour. The sauce is a simple Mediterranean tomato sauce and it's very versatile – you can change the basil to fresh thyme or tarragon if you fancy a change of flavour. Delicious served with vegetables and rice, or toss the sauce through tagliatelle pasta and serve the salmon fillet on top.

SERVES 4

4 x 120g skinless and boneless salmon or trout fillets, from a sustainable source
1 tbsp olive oil, plus a drizzle
3 garlic cloves, minced
½ tsp chilli flakes
60ml dry white wine or vermouth
1 x 400g tin cherry tomatoes
½ tsp sugar
3 tbsp double cream
1 tbsp chopped flat-leaf parsley
a small handful of basil leaves, shredded, plus a few extra whole leaves to serve
½ lemon, for squeezing
sea salt and freshly ground black pepper

Season the salmon fillets with salt and black pepper on both sides. Heat the oil in a large frying pan over a medium heat and add the salmon. Cook for 2–3 minutes on each side or until just cooked through. Remove from the pan and set aside.

Add a drizzle of oil to the pan and add the garlic and chilli flakes. Cook for 30 seconds until fragrant. Add the wine and bubble off the alcohol for 1 minute, then add the tomatoes. Stir in the sugar and bring to the boil, then simmer gently for 5–6 minutes.

Reduce the heat and stir in the cream, parsley and basil. Season to taste with salt and pepper. Return the salmon to the pan to warm through for a minute or two, basting the fish with the sauce. Serve immediately with a squeeze of lemon and scattered with basil leaves.

Scampi Tacos with Tartare Radish Slaw, Pea Guacamole & Quick Pickled Onion

Sharing a platter of tacos with family or friends is always a fun and enjoyable way to eat a meal. Here's my twist on a chip shop favourite – scampi, peas and tartare sauce. The ingredients list looks a little long, but this is so easy to make using shop-bought scampi (always look for sustainably sourced) which works so well with the chilli-spiked tangy slaw. The scampi can be swapped for fish goujons or even fish fingers!

SERVES 4

1 x 400g bag jumbo wholetail breaded scampi
6–8 soft corn tortillas
sea salt and freshly ground black pepper
lemon wedges, to serve

For the quick pickled onion
½ red onion, thinly sliced
2 tsp lemon juice
1 tbsp apple cider vinegar
2 tsp caster sugar
¼ tsp sea salt

For the tartare radish slaw
3 tbsp low-fat Greek yoghurt
1 tbsp mayonnaise
1 tbsp finely chopped capers
1 tbsp finely chopped gherkins or cornichons
1 medium-hot red chilli, de-seeded and finely chopped
1 tbsp finely chopped flat-leaf parsley
½ lemon, for squeezing
80g radishes, trimmed and finely sliced
250g white cabbage, shredded
1 spring onion, trimmed and finely sliced

For the pea guacamole
100g frozen petits pois, defrosted
1 small garlic clove, chopped
1 tbsp chopped mint leaves
1 large ripe avocado, peeled, stoned and chopped
1 tsp extra-virgin olive oil
juice of ½ lemon

First, make the quick pickled onion. Put the red onion in a sieve and slowly pour over a full kettle of boiling water. Drain well. In a small bowl, mix together the lemon juice, vinegar, sugar and salt, then add the onion. Mix well then set aside to pickle while you make the tacos.

Cook the scampi according to the packet instructions, until nice and crispy.

Meanwhile, make the tartare radish slaw. In a bowl, mix together the yoghurt, mayonnaise, chopped capers, gherkins, chilli and parsley, and stir in lemon juice to taste. Season with salt and pepper. Add the radish, cabbage and spring onion and mix well to coat in the dressing. Check for seasoning and lemon juice.

For the pea guacamole, put the peas, garlic and mint in a food processor and pulse a few times to combine. Add the avocado and oil, then pulse again until combined but still with texture. Season with salt and pepper, and add lemon juice to taste. Transfer to a bowl.

Warm the tortillas in the oven or microwave, according to the packet instructions, or heat on a griddle if you prefer them slightly chargrilled. Season the scampi and drain the pickled onion.

Arrange the scampi, tortillas and accompaniments on a serving board or platter. To serve, fill a tortilla with slaw and add some crispy scampi. Squeeze over a little lemon juice. Top with pea and avocado guacamole and some pickled onion. Enjoy!

Miso, Lime & Ginger Baked Fish Parcels with Sesame Pak Choi

Fish works so well with the umami flavours of miso and the Japanese rice wine, mirin. I've used white miso because it's slightly milder and has a salty, sweet flavour that's great with the fish and punchy ginger. Pak choi is a wonderfully nutritious and crunchy leafy green that makes a deliciously light side dish. This also works well with salmon.

SERVES 4

4 x 150g skinless and boneless cod loin or fillets (or similar white fish), from a sustainable source
½ lime, sliced, plus extra wedges to serve
1 large medium-hot red chilli, de-seeded and finely sliced into rings
3 spring onions, trimmed and finely sliced
steamed rice, to serve

For the marinade
4 tbsp white miso paste
2½ tbsp mirin or rice wine
1 tbsp light soy sauce or tamari
2 tsp runny honey or light brown sugar
zest and juice of ½ lime
1 tsp toasted sesame oil
5cm piece of fresh root ginger, peeled and cut into thin matchsticks

For the sesame pak choi
1 tbsp groundnut or sunflower oil
1 tbsp toasted sesame oil
2 tbsp light soy sauce
3cm piece of fresh root ginger, peeled and grated
1 garlic clove, sliced
4 large pak choi (about 450g in total), leaves separated and washed
1 tsp sesame seeds, toasted

For the marinade, put all the ingredients, keeping back half the ginger, in a bowl and whisk together until well combined. Put the fish fillets in a shallow dish and pour the marinade over the top, turning to coat. Leave to marinate for 20 minutes.

Preheat the oven to 200°C/180°C fan/gas 6. Prepare 4 squares each of foil and baking parchment, large enough to enclose the fish fillets when in parcels (about 35cm square).

Lay out the pieces of foil and place the baking parchment on top. Place a fish fillet in the centre of each and spoon over any leftover marinade. Top with a slice of lime and scatter with the remaining ginger, half the chilli and half the spring onions. Loosely fold the foil around the parchment paper, leaving room for the fish to steam while sealing the parcels tightly to enclose the filling. Place on a baking tray and bake for 16–20 minutes, depending on the thickness of the fillets, until the fish is cooked through. Check at 16 minutes: the flesh will flake easily when cooked.

Meanwhile, heat the groundnut oil in a wok or sauté pan that has a lid over a medium heat and add half the sesame oil, half the soy sauce, the ginger, garlic and pak choi. Toss until coated then cover, reduce the heat to low and cook for 2–3 minutes, tossing occasionally, until the leaves have wilted but the stalks still have some bite. Season with the remaining sesame oil and soy sauce. Sprinkle over the toasted sesame seeds.

Unwrap the fish parcels, remove the fish to a plate and spoon over any cooking juices. Sprinkle with the remaining chilli and spring onion. Serve with steamed rice, with the pak choi on the side and lime wedges for squeezing.

Big Flava Fish Cakes with Sweetcorn Salsa

These moreish fish cakes are great for an easy lunch or supper – they're nice and light with a hint of Caribbean spice, and my quick sweetcorn salsa is a fresh and zingy accompaniment. You can oven bake the fish cakes if you prefer, see Note below.

SERVES 4

400g skinless and boneless firm white fish, from a sustainable source
500g floury potatoes, peeled and cut into chunks
sunflower oil, for frying
3cm piece of fresh root ginger, peeled and finely grated
½ Scotch bonnet chilli, de-seeded and finely chopped (optional)
2 spring onions, trimmed and finely sliced, whites and greens separated
2–3 tsp mild Caribbean curry powder, according to taste
2 tbsp finely chopped coriander leaves
zest and juice of ½ lime
3 tbsp gram (chickpea) flour
sea salt and freshly ground black pepper

For the sweetcorn salsa
1 x 198g tin sweetcorn, drained and rinsed
a pinch of cayenne
1 red pepper, de-seeded and diced
½ red onion, finely chopped
2 tomatoes, de-seeded and diced
a handful of coriander leaves, chopped
1 tbsp chopped mint leaves
1 tsp snipped chives
zest and juice of ½ lime
1 tsp honey or maple syrup
olive oil, for drizzling

To serve
mayonnaise (spiked with a dash of hot sauce)
lime wedges

Poach the fish or bake in a lightly oiled foil parcel (14–16 minutes at 200°C/180°C fan/gas 6) until just cooked through, but still nice and moist. When cool enough to handle, break into chunks, being careful to remove any remaining bones.

Meanwhile, boil the potatoes in a large pan of salted water for 10–12 minutes or until tender. Drain well and leave in the colander to steam dry. Tip into a large bowl and lightly mash with the back of a fork or masher, leaving it a bit chunky.

Heat 1 tablespoon of oil in a frying pan over a medium heat and add the ginger, chilli (if using), spring onion whites and curry powder. Cook for 1 minute then tip into the bowl with the potato. Add the coriander, spring onion greens, lime zest and a good squeeze of lime juice, and mix well. Flake in the fish, season with ½ teaspoon of salt and a good grind of pepper and mix until well combined.

Use your hands to divide the mixture into 8 even portions. Lightly squeeze and shape into balls and then gently flatten into fish cakes. Place on a lightly oiled plate, cover and chill in the fridge to firm up for 15–20 minutes.

Meanwhile, place the sweetcorn in a bowl with all of the remaining salsa ingredients and toss together with a drizzle of olive oil. Season with salt and pepper.

Lightly dust the fishcakes with the gram flour. Heat 2 tablespoons of oil in a frying pan over a medium heat and fry the fish cakes for 3–4 minutes on each side until golden brown and completely warmed through (if they are browning too quickly, reduce the heat).

Serve immediately with the corn salsa, mayonnaise and lime wedges for squeezing.

NOTE

To oven-bake the fish cakes, omit the dusting in gram flour and spray a little oil onto a parchment-lined baking sheet. Arrange the fish cakes on top, spray with a little more oil and bake for 25–30 minutes at 200°C/180°C fan/gas 6, until crisp and golden.

Pan-Fried Sea Bass with Broccoli & Roasted Red Pepper & Almond Sauce

This colourful fish dish is full of fresh and punchy flavours – perfect for a delicious dinner for two. The sea bass is simply cooked, just as it should be, and served with a lightly smoked pepper sauce and nutty greens. If you prefer, you can use trout or mackerel fillets. Great with my sweet potato wedges (page 216). For another day, stir the red pepper sauce through some pasta or gnocchi for a tasty, quick meal.

SERVES 2

220g broccoli florets or
 Tenderstem broccoli,
 thick stems trimmed
1–2 tbsp extra-virgin
 olive oil
2 sea bass fillets (about
 100g each), line-caught/
 from a sustainable source
light olive oil, for frying
20g flaked almonds, toasted
sea salt and freshly ground
 black pepper
lemon wedges, to serve

*For the roasted red pepper
 and almond sauce*
20g blanched almonds
3–4 roasted red peppers
 from a jar (about 240g
 in total), drained
1 garlic clove, peeled
 and chopped
¼ tsp smoked paprika
¼ tsp cayenne
1 tbsp chopped flat-leaf
 parsley leaves
2 tsp sherry vinegar
 or red wine vinegar
3–4 tbsp extra-virgin
 olive oil
½ lemon, for squeezing
honey or sugar (optional;
 to taste)

First, make the sauce. In a dry frying pan over a medium heat, toast the blanched almonds for a couple of minutes until lightly toasted. Keep an eye on them as they can easily burn. Tip into a food processor and blitz until finely ground. Add the peppers, garlic, paprika, cayenne, parsley and vinegar and blitz until you have a paste. With the motor running, drizzle in enough olive oil to make a slightly thick but smooth sauce. Season with salt and pepper and add lemon juice to taste. If you like a slightly sweeter sauce, add a little honey or pinch of sugar. Pour into a small saucepan and warm gently over a low heat; keep warm.

Bring a large pan of salted water to the boil. Add the broccoli and cook for 3–4 minutes or until just tender. Drain well and return to the pan, drizzle with extra-virgin olive oil, toss and season with salt and pepper. Keep warm.

Lightly score the skin of the sea bass, using a sharp knife. Drizzle a little light oil on both sides of the fillets and season. Heat a frying pan over a medium heat and, when hot, add the fillets skin-side down. Cook for 3–4 minutes until the skin is golden then carefully turn to cook the other side for 1 minute or until the fish is cooked through and opaque.

To serve, spoon some red pepper sauce onto plates and place the fish on top. Toss the flaked almonds through the broccoli and arrange on the plates alongside the fish. Serve with lemon wedges for squeezing.

Hot-Smoked Trout & Watercress Tart

This tart is simple to make and is an impressive meal to serve to lunch guests or for summer al fresco dining. Smoked trout or salmon is readily available in supermarkets and works so well with peppery watercress. It's at its best served warm (try a slice with a little horseradish and cooked beetroot on the side – it's delightful!) but I also like to wrap up cold slices to take on picnics.

SERVES 6

15g butter
2 banana shallots, peeled and thinly sliced into rings
4 large eggs
2 egg yolks
300ml double cream
a pinch each of sea salt and ground white pepper
zest of 1 large lemon
80g watercress, any thick stalks removed
180g hot-smoked boneless trout or salmon, from a sustainable source

For the pastry
200g plain flour, plus extra for dusting
a pinch of salt
100g cold butter, diced
½ lemon, for squeezing
3–5 tbsp cold water

First, make the pastry. Place the flour and salt in a mixing bowl and add the butter. Using your fingertips, rub together until the mixture resembles fine breadcrumbs. Add a squeeze of lemon and 3 tablespoons water. Using your hands, work the liquid into the flour, adding a little more water if required, until the pastry comes together and forms a ball. Remove from the bowl, wrap in clingfilm and chill in the fridge for 30 minutes.

Preheat the oven to 200°C/180°C fan/gas 6.

Roll the pastry out on a lightly floured work surface to a 3mm thickness. Line a 23cm loose-bottomed tart tin with the pastry, leaving the excess hanging over the edge. Prick the base with a fork. Line the pastry case with baking parchment and fill with baking beans. Bake blind for 15 minutes, then remove the baking beans. Return to the oven for 8–10 minutes until the pastry is cooked through. Use a small, sharp knife to trim away the excess pastry from the edge of the case. Reduce the oven temperature to 180°C/160°C fan/gas 4.

Meanwhile, in a frying pan over a low-medium heat, add the butter and cook the shallots for 3–4 minutes until soft but not coloured. In a bowl, beat the eggs and yolks with the cream, season with a good pinch of sea salt and white pepper and add the lemon zest.

Spoon the shallots into the cooked pastry case and scatter over the watercress. Remove any skin from the trout and flake the fish over the top of the watercress. Pour over the eggs and cream. Bake for 30–35 minutes or until the filling is just set and golden. Leave the tart to cool in the tin for 10 minutes before turning out and slicing.

Fabulous Fish Pie

This is a homely and satisfying fish pie that's simple to prepare and great for a family dinner. You can use any combination of firm-fleshed fish you like, and many supermarkets sell ready prepped fish pie mixes, although I always like to include some smoked haddock for a depth of flavour. You can make the pie ahead of time and cook from chilled – just bake for 40–45 minutes until completely heated through. Try with my Vichy-Style Carrots (page 217).

SERVES 4–6

1kg floury potatoes, peeled and cut into chunks
700ml full-fat milk
1 bay leaf
650g mixture of skinless and boneless firm fish, large pieces, from a sustainable source
2 heaped tbsp crème fraîche
100g butter, plus extra for greasing
1 leek, trimmed and thinly sliced
50g plain flour
1 heaped tsp English or Dijon mustard
zest and juice of ½ lemon
3 tbsp chopped flat-leaf parsley, plus extra to serve
1 tsp snipped chives
150g raw tiger or king prawns, from a sustainable source
a handful of frozen peas, defrosted
50g Cheddar, grated (optional)
sea salt and ground white pepper

Preheat the oven to 200°C/180°C fan/gas 6.

Put the potatoes in a large pan of salted boiling water, cover and simmer for 15–20 minutes or until tender.

Meanwhile, put the milk and bay leaf in a deep-sided frying pan, season and slowly bring to the boil over a medium heat. Add the fish fillets, then reduce the heat and gently poach for 4–6 minutes. Using a slotted spoon, lift the fish onto a plate to cool slightly. When cool enough to handle, check for any stray bones, keeping the fish in large chunks. Strain the milk into a jug.

Drain the cooked potatoes and allow to steam in the colander for a few minutes to dry out. Tip back into the pan and mash the potatoes well with a potato masher or pass through a ricer for super-smooth mash. Beat in the crème fraîche and half the butter and season with salt and white pepper.

Melt the remaining butter in a saucepan over a low-medium heat. Add the leeks and cook for 6–8 minutes until softened but not coloured. Increase the heat to medium, stir in the flour and cook, stirring, for 1–2 minutes. Gradually pour in the reserved milk, whisking constantly, then simmer over a low heat for 6–8 minutes, stirring occasionally until thickened. Stir in the mustard, lemon zest and a small squeeze of juice, and check for seasoning. Add the parsley, chives, prawns and peas.

Lightly grease a deep ovenproof pie dish or medium lasagne dish with butter. Add the fish then spoon over the sauce to cover. Let rest for a few minutes to allow a slight skin to form, then spoon or pipe over the potatoes to cover completely. Smooth with a spatula (unless piped) and scrape the surface with a fork to fluff the surface slightly. Scatter over the grated cheese (if using) and bake for 20–25 minutes or until heated through and the top is golden.

Serve garnished with some fresh parsley.

Keralan Fish & King Prawn Curry

Originating from the south coast of India, this fragrant fish and coconut curry is one of my favourites to serve to friends and family. It's quick and simple to make once you have all the spices ready, and it's full of flavour and sure to impress. If you want a creamier sauce, stir in a 160ml tin of coconut cream with the coconut milk. Serve with basmati rice or try my coriander flatbreads (page 170).

SERVES 4

1 tsp Kashmiri chilli powder or sweet paprika (unsmoked)
1 tsp ground turmeric
zest and juice of 1 lime
500g skinless and boneless firm white fish, from a sustainable source, cut into 4cm pieces
165g raw shelled king prawns, deveined if necessary, from a sustainable source
1 tsp black peppercorns
1 tsp fenugreek seeds
1 tsp coriander seeds
½ tsp cumin seeds
1–2 green chillies, de-seeded and chopped
2 tbsp coconut or groundnut oil
1 heaped tsp mustard seeds
15–20 curry leaves (preferably fresh)
1 onion, finely chopped
4 garlic cloves, minced
5cm piece of fresh root ginger, peeled and finely chopped
1 x 400ml tin coconut milk
2 tbsp chopped coriander, plus extra to serve
sea salt and freshly ground black pepper
lime wedges, to serve

In a bowl, mix together half the chilli powder, half the turmeric, the lime zest, half the juice and a small pinch of salt. Add the fish and prawns and leave to marinate while you get on with the curry.

Toast the peppercorns, fenugreek, coriander and cumin seeds in a dry frying pan over a medium heat for 60 seconds until fragrant. Remove from the heat and grind in a pestle and mortar to a powder. Add the remaining chilli powder and turmeric, half the green chilli and a pinch of salt and grind together. Add a little water and pound until you have a paste. Set aside.

Heat the oil in a large sauté or deep-sided frying pan over a medium heat and add the mustard seeds, curry leaves and the remaining green chilli. Cook for 20 seconds until the seeds sizzle and pop. Add the onion, garlic and ginger and cook for 8–10 minutes until softened and lightly coloured. Stir in the spice paste and cook for another 2–3 minutes, adding a splash of water if needed. Stir in the coconut milk and simmer for 4 minutes to allow the flavours to infuse. Add the fish, prawns and any marinade. Season and bring to a simmer. Cook gently over a low-medium heat for 5–7 minutes or until the fish is cooked through and flakes easily. Stir through the coriander and remaining lime juice and check the seasoning.

Scatter with coriander and serve immediately with a side of basmati rice and lime wedges for squeezing.

Beer-Battered Fish with Triple-Cooked Chips & Mushy Minty Peas

Fish and chips is one of life's greatest pleasures! This is a British classic with a beer batter that's crispy and tasty and keeps the fish moist on the inside. If you prefer, pop the chips in the oven to bake at 220°C/200°C fan/gas 7 for 18–20 minutes after boiling, but they won't be quite as crispy as the triple-cooked.

SERVES 4

1.5kg Maris Piper or Russet potatoes, peeled and cut into chunky chips
4 x 175g skinless and boneless white fish fillets (pollock, haddock, cod), from a sustainable source
½ lemon, for squeezing
250g plain flour, plus extra for dusting
½ tsp sea salt
2 tsp baking powder
a good pinch of cayenne
300–330ml cold beer
sunflower or vegetable oil, for deep-frying
sea salt and freshly ground black pepper

For the mushy minty peas
400g peas (defrosted if frozen)
40g butter
6–8 mint leaves, chopped
½ medium-hot fresh chilli, de-seeded and chopped

To serve
lemon wedges or vinegar
your sauce of choice for dipping

Rinse the chips under cold running water then place in a large pan of salted cold water and bring to the boil over a medium heat. Cook for 4–6 minutes or until just tender, then drain well and set aside.

Pat the fish dry, squeeze over a little lemon juice and lightly season with salt and pepper. Lightly dust the fillets with flour.

Sift the flour, salt, baking powder and cayenne into a large bowl. Stirring continuously with a whisk, gradually add enough beer to make a thick, shiny batter (you may not need all the beer).

In a small saucepan over a medium heat, bring just enough water to cover the peas to the boil. Add the peas and cook for 2–3 minutes until tender. Drain, reserving a little of the cooking water, and place the peas in a food processor. Add the butter, a tablespoon of the reserved cooking water, the mint and chilli and pulse until you reach the desired consistency, adding a little more cooking liquid if needed. Season to taste and keep warm.

Heat enough oil for deep-frying in a deep-fryer or deep heavy-based saucepan, making sure it comes no more than two-thirds of the way up the saucepan, to 180°C. If you don't have a thermometer, test with a drop of batter: it should sizzle and crisp immediately.

Pat the chips dry with a clean tea towel or kitchen paper and gently add to the hot oil. Fry for 3–5 minutes until just starting to colour. Remove and drain well on kitchen paper.

Dip the floured fish in the batter, making sure it is well covered. Carefully lower the fish 1 or 2 at a time into the hot oil and cook for 6–8 minutes, depending on thickness, until crisp and golden. Remove, drain on kitchen paper, season with salt and keep warm.

Return the chips to the hot oil and fry for 3 minutes or until crisp and golden. Drain well on kitchen paper and season with salt.

Serve the fish hot with the chips and mushy minty peas, with lemon wedges or vinegar and your favourite sauce for dipping.

Pan-Seared Sardines with Thyme-Roasted Vine Tomato & Bread Salad

I've always loved sardines on toast, and when I was a young chef it was one of my go-to meals when I got in from a long shift. Food can be so evocative, and now whenever I eat sardines I'm always reminded of those times. Here I've taken the flavours of that simple enjoyable snack and elevated them to make a scrumptious summery salad that's perfect for lunch or a light supper. You can buy butterflied sardine fillets – often Cornish – from most supermarkets. They're good value and also save you from messing around with too many bones. For ease, you can use a good-quality tin of sardines if you prefer.

**SERVES 2
(OR 4 AS A STARTER)**

6 ripe, medium vine tomatoes, halved
1 tsp sugar
¼–½ tsp chilli flakes
2 tsp fresh thyme leaves
1 tbsp sherry vinegar
3–4 tbsp extra-virgin olive oil, plus extra to finish
150g sourdough or rustic bread, torn or cut into cubes
2–4 butterflied sardine fillets, checked for bones, from a sustainable source
oil, for brushing
a handful of basil leaves, shredded
a handful of flat-leaf parsley leaves, roughly chopped
zest and juice of ½ lemon
a large handful of rocket leaves
sea salt and freshly ground black pepper

Preheat the oven to 180°C/160°C fan/gas 4.

Arrange the tomatoes cut-side up in a single layer in a large roasting tray. Sprinkle over ¼ teaspoon of salt, the sugar, chilli flakes and half the thyme leaves. Drizzle with the vinegar and 1–2 tablespoons of the extra-virgin olive oil. Roast on the top shelf of the oven for 30–35 minutes until the tomatoes have softened.

Meanwhile, place the bread chunks in a second roasting tray and drizzle with 2 tablespoons of extra-virgin olive oil, season with salt and sprinkle over the remaining thyme. Toss to coat, then arrange in a single layer and roast on the middle shelf of the oven for 12–15 minutes until the bread is crunchy and lightly toasted.

Towards the end of the tomato and bread cooking time, prepare the sardines. Season the fillets on both sides with salt. Brush a non-stick frying pan with oil and heat until very hot. Add the sardines and cook, skin-side down, for 2–3 minutes until golden. Gently turn the fillets over and cook the other side for 40–60 seconds or until cooked through.

Arrange the roasted tomatoes on serving plates. Toss the toasted bread through any juices in the tomato roasting tray then arrange on the plates over the tomatoes. Place the sardines on top and scatter with the herbs. Sprinkle with lemon zest and squeeze over some juice. Top with rocket leaves and finish with a little drizzle of extra-virgin olive oil and a grind of pepper. Serve immediately.

Quick Peppered Mackerel Kedgeree with Mint Yoghurt

This tasty rice dish is a quick and simple version of a kedgeree using peppered smoked mackerel fillets; something I often have in the fridge because they're versatile and great value for money. It's fab for a lazy brunch, light lunch or quick and satisfying supper. You can also use packets of microwaveable rice or leftover rice to make this even easier – just add to the pan after the spices (omitting the stock) and before flaking in the fish.

SERVES 4

a drizzle of oil
1 tsp mustard seeds
4 spring onions, trimmed
   and sliced, greens and
   whites separated
4cm piece of fresh root
   ginger, peeled and grated
1 medium-hot red chilli,
   de-seeded and finely
   chopped (optional)
1 tbsp butter
1½ tbsp mild curry powder
350g basmati rice,
   well rinsed
600ml chicken or
   vegetable stock
3 eggs
1 pack of peppered smoked
   mackerel (about 3 fillets),
   skin removed, flaked into
   bite-sized pieces
8–10 cherry tomatoes,
   halved
a handful of coriander,
   roughly chopped,
   plus extra to serve
1 lemon, cut into wedges,
   for squeezing and to serve
sea salt

For the mint yoghurt
120g natural yoghurt
1 medium-hot red chilli,
   de-seeded and finely
   chopped (optional)
1 tbsp finely chopped mint

First, make the mint yoghurt. In a small bowl, mix together the yoghurt, chilli (if using) and mint. Season with a little salt and chill until ready to serve.

Heat the oil in a deep-sided lidded frying pan over a medium heat and add the mustard seeds. When they start to pop, add the spring onion whites, ginger, chilli (if using) and a pinch of salt and cook for 1 minute before adding the butter and curry powder. Cook through for 30 seconds until fragrant. Stir through the rice for a minute until coated in all the spices. Add the stock, cover with a tight-fitting lid and cook over a low heat for 12 minutes or until the rice is cooked through.

Meanwhile, cook the eggs in a saucepan of boiling water for 8 minutes. Rinse in cold water until cool enough to handle. Peel and set aside.

Remove the lid from the rice and gently fork through. Add the flaked mackerel, the spring onion greens and the tomatoes. Cover and cook for 2–3 minutes to warm through. Check the seasoning and stir through the coriander and a squeeze of lemon.

Cut the eggs into quarters and serve on top of the rice with a good scattering of coriander, lemon wedges and the mint yoghurt.

Salmon, Roasted Tenderstem & Potato Traybake with Watercress Sauce

Traybakes are brilliant for mid-week cooking and this effortless salmon bake with a vibrant fresh green sauce from peppery watercress is the perfect fuss-free meal. It also looks rather colourful on the plate. When in season, I love to throw in a handful of lightly blanched samphire with the capers, for a real taste of the sea. Equally delicious with trout fillets.

SERVES 4

700g Fingerling, Anya or small waxy potatoes, scrubbed and halved lengthways
2 tbsp olive oil, plus extra for drizzling
300g Tenderstem broccoli, thick stems trimmed
1 garlic clove, minced
4 x 120g salmon or trout fillets, from a sustainable source
½ lemon, for squeezing
1 tbsp capers, drained and rinsed
2 tbsp pine nuts or almond slivers, toasted (optional)
sea salt and freshly ground black pepper

For the watercress sauce
60g watercress, plus extra to serve
5g fresh dill (or tarragon or chives)
140g crème fraîche
zest and juice of ½ lemon
1–2 tbsp extra-virgin olive oil

Preheat the oven to 200°C/180°C fan/gas 6.

First, make the sauce. Put the watercress and dill into a food processor and blitz until finely chopped. Add the crème fraîche, lemon zest and juice, 1 tablespoon of extra-virgin olive oil and a good pinch each of salt and pepper. Blend until you have a vibrant green, pourable sauce, adding another tablespoon of oil if needed. Chill until needed.

Spread the potatoes out in a large, non-stick baking tray lined with baking parchment. Drizzle over the oil and add a good pinch of salt. Toss to coat then roast for 20–25 minutes.

Put the Tenderstem broccoli in a bowl, drizzle with a little oil and sprinkle over the garlic. Remove the tray from the oven, add the broccoli and toss through. Lightly oil the fish fillets and season with salt and pepper. Nestle them into the tray in between the vegetables and squeeze over some lemon juice. Roast for 12–15 minutes or until the fish is cooked through. Scatter over the capers 2–3 minutes before the end of cooking.

Remove the tray from the oven and sprinkle over the pine nuts (if using) and some watercress leaves. Serve with the watercress sauce for pouring.

Seared Tuna, Mixed Tomato & Bean Salad with Anchovy & Tomato Dressing

This main-course salad is a twist on an Italian tuna and bean salad – it's fresh, nutritious and full of Mediterranean flavour. Fresh tuna is meaty, flavoursome and easy to cook but you can use a good-quality tinned tuna if you prefer – just drain, flake and toss through the salad before dressing. Sun-blushed or sun-soaked tomatoes are sweeter and less intense than sun-dried and they can often be found in the deli section of supermarkets, or you can make your own (see page 215).

SERVES 4

4 x 170g fresh tuna steaks, Albacore or from a sustainable source
2 tbsp olive oil, plus extra for brushing
1 garlic clove, minced
zest and juice of ½ lemon
a pinch of herbes de Provence
150g cherry tomatoes, halved
50g sun-blushed tomatoes, roughly chopped
1 x 400g tin white beans (cannellini/butter beans), drained and rinsed
1 x 400g tin haricot or mixed beans, drained and rinsed
a handful of black olives, pitted and halved
½ red onion, finely sliced
1 tbsp chopped chervil or 2 tsp chopped tarragon
2 tbsp roughly chopped flat-leaf parsley
a handful of rocket leaves
flaky sea salt and freshly ground black pepper

For the dressing
2–3 anchovy fillets in oil, drained and finely chopped
1 small garlic clove, minced
1 large ripe vine tomato
1½ tbsp red wine vinegar
4 tbsp extra-virgin olive oil

Place the tuna in a shallow dish with the oil, garlic, lemon juice, herbes de Provence and a pinch each of salt and pepper. Turn the tuna so that it is well coated, cover and set aside to marinate for 15–20 minutes.

Make the dressing. In a bowl, mash the anchovy with the garlic, using a fork or the back of a spoon. Using a box grater, coarsely grate in the tomato, discarding the skin. Mix in the vinegar and then whisk in the olive oil. Season to taste.

In a large bowl, combine the cherry tomatoes, sun-blushed tomatoes, beans, lemon zest, olives, onion, chervil, parsley and rocket. Stir to combine.

Heat a griddle or frying pan over a medium-high heat and brush with a little oil. Remove the tuna from the marinade and shake off any excess. Cook the tuna for 1–2 minutes on each side or until cooked to your liking – don't overcook or it will become dry. Leave to rest for a couple of minutes and lightly season with salt.

Pour three quarters of the dressing over the bean and tomato salad, toss to combine and divide between four serving plates. Cut each tuna fillet in half and place on top of the salad. Drizzle over the remaining dressing and give it a good grind of black pepper. Serve immediately with some crusty bread.

Zesty Seafood Kebabs with Shaved Courgette & Fennel Salad

These zingy kebabs are simply marinated to allow the flavours of the sea to shine. A pinch of zesty sumac brings a wonderful tang, and the fresh and light courgette salad with a hint of aniseed fennel complements perfectly. When filming the series, I went foraging for sea herbs with Alysia Vasey, and I tossed some sea purslane, aster and sea coriander through the salad. They worked beautifully, so if you like a bit of foraging then give them a try. Scallops are a bit of a treat and are wonderful when cooked on the barbecue, but you can leave them out if you prefer.

SERVES 4–6

3 tbsp olive oil
2 lemons, zest and juice of 1, the other thinly sliced
1 tbsp runny honey
1 tsp chopped dill
2 pinches of sumac
16 raw shelled tiger prawns, deveined if necessary, from a sustainable source
12 prepared fresh scallops, from a sustainable source
400g firm white fish, cut into 2.5cm chunks
1 lime, thinly sliced

For the salad
½ tsp fennel seeds, toasted
3 tbsp extra-virgin olive oil
zest and juice of ½ lemon
2 tsp runny honey
1 tsp chopped dill
3 courgettes, trimmed and shaved into ribbons using a swivel peeler or mandoline
1 small fennel bulb, cored and shaved or thinly sliced, fronds reserved
a large handful of peppery salad leaves (rocket, watercress or mustard)
flaky sea salt and freshly ground black pepper

Mix the oil, lemon zest and juice, honey, dill and a pinch of sumac in a large bowl. Add the seafood and fish and mix well. Cover and leave to marinate for 20 minutes (no longer otherwise the lemon juice will start to 'cook' the fish).

Meanwhile, prepare the salad. Crush the fennel seeds with a pestle and mortar and then whisk together with the extra-virgin olive oil, lemon zest and juice, honey and dill. Season with salt. Put the shaved courgette ribbons and fennel slices into a bowl. Toss through the salad leaves and reserved fennel fronds. When ready to serve, drizzle over the fennel dressing and check the seasoning.

Preheat a barbecue or griddle pan.

Thread the prawns, scallops and fish onto 4–6 skewers, alternating with folded slices of lemon and lime. Season with salt and a pinch of sumac.

Lightly oil the grill of the barbecue or the griddle pan and cook the kebabs over a medium heat for 6–8 minutes or until the fish is cooked through, basting with the marinade and turning once.

Serve the seafood kebabs with the courgette and fennel salad on the side.

Chapter Four
MEAT & POULTRY

Lemon & Herb Chicken Flatties with Celeriac Remoulade

This is a wonderfully simple and appetising meal that's perfect for a light mid-week dinner, weekend lunch or barbecue. Butterflying the chicken breasts ensures they cook quickly and evenly so it's ideal for the chargrill. Celeriac remoulade is a French classic and a great way to serve this under-used vegetable. I love its earthy nuttiness with the rich, creamy dressing, although you can make a healthier version by using half-fat mayo and 0% fat Greek yoghurt if preferred. This probably makes more remoulade than you need but it will keep in the fridge for a couple of days.

SERVES 4

zest and juice of 1 lemon
3 tbsp extra-virgin olive oil, plus extra for drizzing over the rocket
2 garlic cloves, minced
½ tsp chilli flakes (optional)
½ tsp dried mixed herbs
2 tbsp finely chopped fresh herbs (I use lemon thyme, parsley and basil), plus extra to serve
4 skinless and boneless chicken breasts
2 lemons, halved
sea salt and freshly ground black pepper
a small bag (about 60g) rocket (and French fries if you like), to serve

For the remoulade
1 medium celeriac, peeled and cut into thin matchsticks or shredded in a food processor
zest and juice of ½ lemon
3–4 tbsp good-quality mayonnaise
3 tbsp crème fraîche or Greek yoghurt
2 tsp extra-virgin olive oil
1 tbsp grain mustard
2 tbsp finely chopped flat-leaf parsley

In a large shallow dish, whisk together the lemon zest and juice, olive oil, garlic, chilli flakes (if using), dried and fresh herbs and season with ½ teaspoon of salt and a good grind of black pepper.

Put a chicken breast on a chopping board and place your hand on top. Using a sharp knife, carefully slice horizontally down one side but not all the way through. Open the halves like a book to resemble a butterfly. Cover with a piece of baking parchment and lightly bash to flatten. Repeat with the other chicken breasts. Place the butterflied breasts in the dish with the marinade and baste to coat. Cover and chill to marinate for a minimum of 30 minutes or longer if you have the time.

Meanwhile, make the remoulade. Put the celeriac in a large bowl and mix in a squeeze of lemon juice. Mix together the remaining ingredients and then stir through the celeriac until well combined. Season and add a little more mayonnaise or lemon juice if needed. Cover and set aside.

Bring the chicken to room temperature 20 minutes before cooking. Heat a griddle pan over a medium heat (or preheat the barbecue) and cook the chicken for 4 minutes on each side or until cooked through and nicely chargrilled. Add the lemon halves to the pan or barbecue cut-side down for a couple of minutes to char.

Serve the butterflied chicken scattered with fresh herbs, with the remoulade on the side and a handful of rocket lightly dressed with extra-virgin olive oil, and the charred lemon for squeezing over. It's always nice to have a side of French fries too!

Rose Harissa Chicken Tagine with Apricots & Chickpeas

I'm using a ready-made harissa paste to add depth and a smoky chilli kick to my quick and easy tagine. Rose harissa adds a lovely hint of floral sweetness to counter the heat of the chillies and you can add more or less depending on how spicy you like your tagine – you can keep it sweet and mild if cooking for young kids. You can use chicken breasts if you prefer, just adjust the cooking times accordingly. Serve with your favourite couscous.

SERVES 4

6–8 skinless and boneless chicken thighs, cut into quarters

1½ tbsp rose harissa paste

2 tbsp light olive oil or sunflower oil, plus extra for drizzling

1 large onion, roughly chopped

4cm piece of fresh root ginger, peeled and chopped

1 tsp ground cumin

½ tsp ground cinnamon

1 x 400g tin plum or chopped tomatoes

120g ready-to-eat dried apricots, halved

400–450ml chicken stock, hot (infused with a small pinch of saffron, optional)

1 x 400g tin chickpeas, drained and rinsed

1 tbsp runny honey

2 tbsp chopped coriander or parsley, plus extra to serve

½ lemon, for squeezing

sea salt and freshly ground black pepper

Put the chicken in a bowl with ½ tablespoon of the harissa, a pinch of salt and pepper and a drizzle of oil. Rub the paste into the meat, cover and leave to marinate for 20 minutes, or chill to marinate for longer if you have the time.

Heat the oil in a large heavy-based saucepan or flameproof casserole over a medium-high heat, tip in the chicken pieces and cook for a few minutes until lightly browned all over. Carefully remove from the pan with a slotted spoon and set aside. Reduce the heat to medium, adding a little more oil if needed, and fry the onion and ginger for 6–8 minutes, until softened and beginning to brown. Stir through the remaining harissa, the cumin and cinnamon.

Return the chicken to the pan. When the chicken is well coated in the spices, stir in the tomatoes, apricots and 400ml of the stock. Give everything a good stir to scrape all the flavour from the bottom of the pan. Add a good pinch of salt, bring to a simmer and cover. Simmer for 15 minutes, stirring occasionally, adding a little more stock if needed.

Add the chickpeas and 2 teaspoons of the honey and continue to simmer for another 15–20 minutes, uncovered, stirring occasionally and breaking up the plum tomatoes (if using plum) with your spoon, until reduced and slightly thickened. Stir in the coriander, squeeze in some lemon juice and check for seasoning and sweetness, adding the remaining honey if needed.

Sprinkle with coriander and serve with couscous.

Chicken & Spring Vegetable Casserole

Casseroles aren't just for the winter months and they're a great way to enjoy seasonal vegetables. This is a tasty and comforting chicken casserole full of fresh green vegetables and aromatic herbs, and I'm using chicken legs which makes this a great value meal for the whole family to enjoy, but you can use chicken thighs if you prefer. Feel free to mix up the greens – roughly chopped runner or string beans are also great to use. Serve with warm crusty bread for mopping up the juice.

SERVES 4

1 tbsp light olive oil
4 chicken legs, skin-on
    and bone-in
3 smoked bacon rashers,
    roughly chopped
1 onion, chopped
1 celery stick, finely
    chopped
2 garlic cloves, minced
300g new potatoes,
    halved if large
2 lemon thyme sprigs
    (or regular thyme)
1 bay leaf
100ml white wine
400ml chicken stock
150g baby broad beans
    or podded edamame
    (defrosted, if frozen)
200g spring greens or
    young kale, stalks
    removed, shredded
150g frozen petits pois,
    defrosted
2 tbsp chopped flat-leaf
    parsley
2 tbsp double cream
    (optional)
2 tsp snipped chives
zest of ½ lemon
sea salt and freshly
    ground black pepper

Heat the oil in a shallow 30cm-wide flameproof casserole that has a lid over a medium-high heat. Add the chicken skin-side down, reduce the heat to medium and leave to cook for 6–8 minutes or until golden brown (you may need to do this in batches). Turn and cook for another 3–4 minutes until sealed all over. Transfer to a plate. Add the bacon to the pan and cook until lightly browned then add the onion, celery and garlic. Cook for 4–6 minutes until the onion is softened but not coloured.

Add the potatoes, thyme and bay leaf to the pan, then pour in the wine. Allow the wine to bubble and reduce for 1 minute. Stir in the stock and return the chicken to the pan, making sure the chicken is skin-side up. Season with salt and pepper. Half-cover the pan, reduce the heat to low to medium and simmer for 30–35 minutes or until the chicken is cooked through. Remove the chicken and keep warm. Add the beans and spring greens, cover and simmer for 3 minutes then stir in the peas and parsley. Cook without a lid for a further few minutes until the vegetables are tender. Stir in the cream (if using). Check the seasoning. Nestle the chicken back in the pan, sprinkle over the chives and finish with a good grating of lemon zest. Serve at the table with a side of warm crusty bread.

Chicken Kiev with Tarragon & Lemony Beans

Ok, so a garlic-butter-filled chicken covered in breadcrumbs may not be the healthiest meal, but yeah boi, it's good! Chicken Kiev is a timeless classic and although it's a bit retro, it's always a winner for a family dinner. I've added a hint of aromatic anise by using tarragon, which gives a lovely bittersweet flavour to the garlic butter. Serve with a creamy mash (page 216).

SERVES 4

100g salted butter, softened
3 tbsp finely chopped
    flat-leaf parsley
2 tbsp finely chopped
    tarragon
3 garlic cloves, minced
4 large skinless and
    boneless chicken breasts
150g panko breadcrumbs
3 tbsp freshly grated
    Parmesan
4 tbsp plain flour, seasoned
    with a pinch each of
    cayenne and salt
2 eggs, beaten
2–3 tablespoons
    sunflower oil, plus
    extra for greasing
sea salt and freshly
    ground black pepper

For the lemony beans
2 tbsp extra-virgin olive oil
zest and juice of ½ lemon
300g fine green beans,
    trimmed

In a bowl, mash together the butter, parsley, tarragon, garlic and plenty of salt and pepper. Mould into a sausage shape and tightly wrap in clingfilm. Freeze until firm then slice into 8 equal pieces.

Using a small knife, horizontally cut a deep pocket into each chicken breast. Place 2 slices of the chilled butter inside the pocket of each breast and press down, pinching to seal the edges of the chicken and completely covering the butter (use cocktail sticks to secure if needed).

Put the breadcrumbs and Parmesan on a plate and mix together. Put the seasoned flour on another plate and the beaten egg on a third (deep) plate. Coat the chicken breasts in the seasoned flour, dusting off any excess, dip in the beaten egg to get a good coating, then turn to coat in the breadcrumbs. Repeat the process to get a double coating. Chill the chicken breasts for 1 hour before cooking.

Preheat the oven to 200°C/180°C fan/gas 6 and lightly grease a baking tray.

Heat the sunflower oil in a large frying pan over a medium heat and fry the chicken for 2 minutes on each side until golden brown. Transfer to the baking tray and bake in the oven for 18–20 minutes or until cooked through.

Meanwhile, for the beans, in a large bowl mix together the olive oil and lemon zest and juice, and season with salt and pepper. Add the green beans to a saucepan of well salted boiling water and boil for 3–5 minutes until just tender. Drain well then tip into the bowl of dressing. Toss to coat and adjust the seasoning, adding more lemon juice to taste if needed.

Serve the chicken Kiev straight from the oven with the lemony beans and a side of mash.

Herb-Stuffed Roast Chicken Traybake

This is a simple and great value traybake version of a roast chicken dinner and it's perfect for a lazy Sunday. Using skin-on chicken thighs keeps the meat moist and you also get your own fair share of crispy skin!

SERVES 4

25g butter
1 small onion,
    finely chopped
80g breadcrumbs
    (day-old bread is best)
1 lemon, cut into wedges,
    plus the zest of ½
1 tbsp finely chopped
    flat-leaf parsley
3 tsp chopped thyme leaves
8 skin-on boneless
    chicken thighs
1 red onion, peeled
    and cut into wedges
3–4 large Maris Piper
    or Yukon Gold potatoes,
    peeled and chopped
    into 2.5cm chunks
4 large garlic cloves,
    unpeeled
2 rosemary sprigs
olive oil, for drizzling
300g chantenay carrots,
    scrubbed, or large
    carrots, peeled and
    cut into 4cm chunks
2 parsnips, peeled and
    cut into large chunks
1 tbsp runny honey
sea salt and freshly
    ground black pepper

For the gravy (optional)
2 tbsp plain flour
400ml chicken stock, hot
gravy browning or low-salt
    soy sauce (optional)

Preheat the oven to 200°C/180°C fan/gas 6.

Melt the butter in a small frying pan over a medium heat and cook the chopped onion for 4–6 minutes until softened but not coloured. Stir in the breadcrumbs, lemon zest, parsley and 2 teaspoons of the thyme, and season with salt and pepper. Remove from the heat and allow to cool a little.

Flatten out the chicken thighs on a work surface, skin-side down. Divide the stuffing between the thighs and fold over to enclose.

Put the red onion wedges, potatoes, lemon wedges, garlic and rosemary sprigs in a large non-stick roasting tray and drizzle generously with olive oil. Season well and toss to coat. Put the carrots and parsnips in a bowl and drizzle with a little oil and the honey. Season, toss to coat, then add to the tray. Sprinkle over the remaining thyme.

Nestle the chicken thighs onto the tray between the vegetables, skin side up. Don't overcrowd the tray – you want everything to sit in one layer, so use two trays if necessary. Season the chicken skins generously and drizzle with a little oil. Roast for 40–50 minutes or until the chicken skin is crisp and golden and the chicken is cooked through, turning the vegetables and basting the chicken halfway through.

Serve straight from the oven or, if you'd like a gravy, remove the chicken thighs and vegetables from the tray and keep warm. Squeeze the garlic cloves from their skins and the juice from some of the roasted lemon wedges into the tray. Put the tray over a medium heat and stir in the flour for 1 minute. Gradually stir in the stock, scraping the bottom of the pan to lift all the flavour. Let it bubble away for a couple of minutes. Add a few drops of gravy browning or soy sauce to darken the colour, if you like. Season with salt and plenty of black pepper and stir until you have a nicely thickened gravy. Strain into a serving jug and serve alongside the chicken and vegetables.

Peri-Peri Chicken & Charred Chilli-Lime Corn

The Portuguese/southern African sauce peri peri, or piri piri, is a rich, smoky and slightly sweet sauce that marries so well with chicken. Roasting the peppers and chillies beforehand pumps up the flavour but you can skip this bit to save time and if you like things hot, feel free to add more chillies. If it's not BBQ weather, roast the chicken in a 200°C/180°C fan/gas 6 oven for 40–45 minutes until the skin is crispy and the juices run clear.

SERVES 4–6

1–1.5kg bone-in,
    skin-on chicken legs
    (about 6–8 pieces)
4–6 corn cobs
80g butter, softened
1 small red chilli, de-seeded
    and finely chopped
a pinch of cayenne
zest and juice of 1 lime
sea salt and freshly
    ground black pepper

For the marinade
1 small red onion, peeled
    and cut into wedges
2 large red peppers,
    de-seeded and quartered
2–3 tbsp olive oil, plus
    extra for drizzling
½ tsp paprika (unsmoked)
3–6 African bird's-eye
    (piri piri) chillies,
    according to taste
5 garlic cloves, peeled
1 tsp sweet smoked paprika
½ tsp ground allspice
1 tsp dried oregano
8–10 basil leaves, torn
1 tbsp red wine vinegar
    or sherry vinegar
zest and juice of ½ lemon
1 tbsp runny honey
a splash of whisky or
    bourbon (optional)

Preheat the oven to 200°C/180°C fan/gas 6.

Place the red onion and peppers on a baking tray and drizzle with oil. Sprinkle with the paprika and roast for 20–25 minutes, then add the chillies and garlic and toss. Roast for another 10 minutes then remove from the oven and allow to cool.

Rip the stems from the chillies and place the contents of the roasting tray with the remaining marinade ingredients (except the oil) in a food processor or blender, along with ½ teaspoon each of salt and pepper. Blend well. Continue to blend while drizzling in the oil until you have a smooth marinade.

Slash the chicken at intervals with a sharp knife and place in a shallow dish. Pour over the marinade and rub into the meat. Cover and chill for at least 2 hours, preferably overnight.

Meanwhile, boil the corn cobs in a large pan of salted water for 10 minutes. Drain and set aside.

Preheat a barbecue and remove the chicken from the fridge to come up to room temperature.

Remove the chicken from the marinade, shaking off any excess, and place over direct heat for 3–4 minutes on each side to sear. Move to a cooler part of the barbecue and cook, turning and basting with any marinade, for a further 35–45 minutes, or until the juices run clear when the thickest part is pierced with a metal skewer. Remove from the heat and allow to rest for a few minutes.

In a bowl, mash together the butter, chilli, cayenne, lime zest and a good squeeze of juice. Season with salt. Rub the corn cobs with some of the butter (reserving some for serving) and place directly on the grill, turning, for 6–8 minutes or until charred on all sides.

Serve the chicken with the corn on the side with a knob of chilli-lime butter melting over the top.

Chargrilled Chicken & Pineapple Chow Skewers with Fresh Coconut Slaw

This really is tropical sunshine and happiness on a plate! I was inspired by the vibrant flavours of a pineapple chow – a zesty and spicy Caribbean salad – and came up with these mouthwatering and colourful kebabs. Rather than mayonnaise I'm using a sweet-spiced pickled dressing for the slaw, which is delightful with the fresh flavours. Adjust the chilli content to suit your taste – these can be served mild and fruity or hot and spicy.

MAKES 6 SKEWERS

1 x 200ml tin coconut milk
¼–1 Scotch bonnet chilli, de-seeded and chopped
4cm piece of fresh root ginger, peeled and grated
2 garlic cloves, minced
1 tbsp honey
zest and juice of 1 lime
2 tbsp dark soy sauce
a dash of hot pepper sauce
2 tbsp chopped coriander
4 skinless and boneless chicken breasts, cut into 2.5cm pieces
1–2 red peppers, de-seeded and cut into 2.5cm pieces
1 pineapple, peeled, cored and cut into 2.5cm chunks
oil, for spraying or drizzling
sea salt

For the fresh coconut slaw
½ red or white cabbage, shredded
1 red onion, thinly sliced
1 carrot, coarsely grated
4 tbsp apple cider vinegar
3 tbsp sugar
1 Scotch bonnet chilli
4 whole allspice (pimento) berries
1 large papaya, de-seeded and diced
50g coarsely grated fresh coconut (or coconut flakes)
a handful of coriander leaves, chopped
a handful of mint leaves, chopped
½ lime, for squeezing

In a large bowl, mix together the coconut milk, chilli, ginger, garlic, honey, lime zest and juice, soy sauce, hot pepper sauce and half the coriander. Remove a quarter of the marinade and set aside for basting later. Add the chicken to the bowl and toss to coat well. Cover and put in the fridge to marinate for at least 2 hours, preferably overnight.

Meanwhile, for the slaw, put the cabbage, onion and carrot in a large bowl. In a small saucepan, combine the vinegar, sugar, chilli, allspice berries and a pinch of salt. Bring to the boil for a couple of minutes until the sugar has melted. Pour over the cabbage and mix well. Leave to cool, then toss through the remaining ingredients with a good squeeze of lime. Check for seasoning, cover and chill until needed, removing the whole chilli and allspice berries before serving.

Remove the chicken from the fridge 30 minutes before cooking to allow the meat to come up to room temperature.

Preheat a barbecue or griddle pan over a medium-high heat.

Thread the chicken onto 6 skewers, alternating with pieces of red pepper and pineapple. Drizzle or spray with a little oil and place directly on the grill on the hot barbecue or straight onto the griddle pan. Cook for 10–14 minutes, turning and basting with the reserved marinade every few minutes, or until the chicken is cooked through and golden on all sides.

Serve the chicken and pineapple skewers scattered with the remaining coriander, and the slaw on the side. Enjoy with a glass of rum punch!

Allspice Honey Duck with Chicory, Orange & Pomegranate Salad

Duck is a delicious meat when it's cooked correctly and its richness pairs beautifully with fruit and citrus. This Middle Eastern-inspired salad is surprisingly easy to make and is a perfect date-night meal – it looks impressive and tastes wonderful with the sweet and tangy notes of pomegranate. Serve with a side of couscous, if you like.

SERVES 2

2 tbsp pomegranate
  molasses
2 tbsp runny honey
1 tbsp light olive oil
zest and juice of 1 orange
1 tsp ground allspice
2 x 150g duck breasts,
  at room temperature
seeds of ½ pomegranate
sea salt

For the salad
1 little gem lettuce,
  leaves separated
2 small heads of chicory
  (red is nice), leaves
  separated
a handful of watercress
8–10 mint leaves, shredded,
  plus extra to serve
2 spring onions, trimmed
  and thinly sliced
1–2 oranges, peeled
  and segmented

For the dressing
3 tbsp extra-virgin olive oil
½ tbsp pomegranate
  molasses
1 tbsp red wine vinegar
  or sherry vinegar
2 tsp runny honey
a pinch of ground allspice

Put the pomegranate molasses, honey, oil, half the orange zest and 2 tablespoons of juice, and half the allspice into a shallow dish and mix well. Using a sharp knife, score the skin of the duck breasts in a criss-cross pattern, taking care not to cut through to the flesh. Brush a little of the marinade onto the skin. Sit the breasts skin-side up in the marinade, cover and set aside for 30 minutes or chill and marinate for longer if you have the time.

Preheat the oven to 200°C/180°C fan/gas 6.

Remove the duck from the marinade, shaking off any excess and patting the skin dry with kitchen paper. Season generously with salt and sprinkle over the remaining allspice.

Put the duck skin-side down into a cold frying pan, place over a medium-high heat and cook for 7–10 minutes without moving until the fat layer has rendered and the skin has turned golden and crispy. Carefully drain any excess fat from the pan, turn the breasts over and cook for 1 minute to seal the meat. If you're not using an ovenproof pan then transfer the duck to a baking tray or dish, skin-side up. Place in the oven and cook for 5–7 minutes for medium, or longer according to your preference. Remove from the oven, cover loosely with foil and leave to rest for 6–8 minutes while you prepare the salad.

In a small bowl, mix together the dressing ingredients with the remaining orange zest and 1 tablespoon of juice. Season with a little salt and stir in half the pomegranate seeds.

Put the salad ingredients into a large bowl and drizzle over some of the dressing. Gently toss to coat.

Thinly slice the duck breasts. Arrange the salad on serving plates and add the duck slices. Drizzle with a little more dressing and scatter with mint leaves and the remaining pomegranate seeds. Serve immediately.

Beef & Mozzarella Rigatoni Bake with Pesto Crumb

Everyone loves a pasta bake – they're easy to make and satisfying to eat. This beef and mozzarella bake is packed full of Italian flavour and I love the crispy texture from the pesto topping. This is definitely one to add to your mid-week meal repertoire.

SERVES 6

2 tbsp olive oil, plus extra for drizzling
1 large onion, finely chopped
1 tsp dried oregano
500g minced beef
1 tsp tomato purée
1 bay leaf
350ml beef stock
1 x 400g tin chopped tomatoes
½ tsp sugar
360g dried rigatoni pasta (or other large pasta shape)
1 x 125g ball mozzarella, torn into pieces
75g fresh breadcrumbs
30g Parmesan, grated
1 tbsp good-quality basil pesto
sea salt and freshly ground black pepper
fresh basil leaves, shredded, to serve

Heat the oil in a large deep-sided frying pan or sauté pan over a medium heat and cook the onion for 4–6 minutes until softened but not coloured. Add the oregano and cook for 30 seconds until fragrant. Stir in the minced beef, season generously with salt and pepper and cook, breaking up the meat with a spoon, until browned all over. Mix in the tomato purée and cook for 1 minute. Stir in the bay leaf, stock, chopped tomatoes and sugar. Bring to the boil then reduce the heat, part cover and simmer gently for 20–25 minutes.

Preheat the oven to 200°C/180°C fan/gas 6.

In a large saucepan of salted water, cook the pasta for 2 minutes less than the packet instructions, until just al dente – don't overcook because it will cook further in the oven. Drain well then mix through the meat sauce.

Transfer to a large baking dish and dot over the mozzarella.

In a bowl, mix together the breadcrumbs, Parmesan and pesto (it's easier to use your fingers) and scatter over the top of the pasta. Drizzle with a little oil and bake in the oven for 25 minutes or until bubbling and golden.

Scatter over the basil leaves to serve.

Peppered Steak with Peppercorn Sauce & Rosemary Oven Chips

This is an old favourite, which is always my go-to for a special occasion. It's easy to make and sure to put you in a good mood, and a little splash of brandy always helps! If you can't find green peppercorns in brine you can soak the dried version in hot salted water or stock for 40 minutes and then drain.

SERVES 2

2 tsp black peppercorns
1 tsp white peppercorns
650g Desiree or Maris Piper potatoes, scrubbed and cut into 1cm-thick chips
2 tbsp light olive oil, plus extra for drizzling
2 large rosemary sprigs, leaves picked and chopped
200g asparagus spears, trimmed
50g butter, plus an extra knob
2 x 200g sirloin steaks
2 shallots, finely chopped
2 tsp green peppercorns in brine, rinsed
2 tbsp brandy or cognac
150ml beef stock
2 tsp Dijon mustard
100ml double cream
1 tbsp chopped flat-leaf parsley
sea salt

Preheat the oven to 250°C/230°C fan/Gas 9.

Put the black and white peppercorns into a pestle and mortar and crush together until coarse. Set aside.

Place the potato chips in a saucepan of salted boiling water and blanch for 3–4 minutes. Drain well and leave in the colander to steam dry for a few minutes then place on a non-stick baking tray and drizzle generously with oil. Season with salt and sprinkle over the rosemary. Toss to ensure each chip is coated in oil. Bake for 16–20 minutes, turning once or twice, until golden and crispy.

Meanwhile, put the asparagus and a knob of butter in a sauté pan over a medium-high heat, just cover with water and add a good pinch of salt. Cook for 4–5 minutes until tender. Keep warm.

Season the steaks with salt then rub the crushed pepper mix over both sides. Drizzle with oil. Place a large frying pan over a high heat until just beginning to smoke. When hot, add the steaks, reduce the heat to medium-high and cook for 1 minute. Turn the steaks and cook for another minute. Reduce the heat to medium, add half the butter and cook, basting constantly with the pan juices, for a further 2–3 minutes, depending on the thickness of your steaks, for medium, or until cooked to your liking. Remove from the pan to rest, keeping warm while you finish the sauce.

Melt the remaining butter in the frying pan, then add the shallots and cook for 30 seconds without colouring. Add the green peppercorns and stir through. Add the brandy and set it alight (if you're feeling brave!). Increase the heat and add the stock and mustard and bring to the boil. Allow it to bubble away until it reduces by half, then stir in the cream and cook for 1–2 minutes to thicken. Stir in the parsley and season with salt to taste.

Serve the steaks with the sauce spooned over and the rosemary chips and asparagus on the side.

Steak & Ale Puff Pastry Pie

A great pie is pure joy and comfort! Steak and ale pie is one of the country's favourites and it's easy to see why. Tender beef, beer and pastry – what's not to like?! Hap-pie eating!

SERVES 4–6

30g plain flour, plus
  extra for dusting
900g stewing or braising
  steak, cut into large
  chunks
3 tbsp light olive oil,
  plus extra if needed
350ml beef stock
30g butter
200g button mushrooms,
  wiped
2 onions, roughly chopped
2 carrots, peeled and
  roughly chopped
3 garlic cloves, minced
2 tsp fresh thyme leaves
2 tsp tomato purée
350ml good-quality dark ale
2 tsp brown sugar
2 bay leaves
2 tbsp Worcestershire sauce
1 x 500g block ready-made
  puff pastry
1 egg, beaten with a
  little milk, to glaze
sea salt and freshly
  ground black pepper

Put the flour into a bowl, season with salt and pepper and add the beef. Toss well until all the pieces are coated.

Heat 2 tablespoons of the oil in a flameproof casserole, add the beef and fry over a high heat for 3–4 minutes until browned. Transfer to a bowl and set aside. Add a splash of stock to the pan and scrape up any sediment. Tip in with the meat and wipe out the pan.

Add half the butter and the mushrooms to the pan and fry over a high heat for 2–3 minutes. Remove with a slotted spoon and set aside. Add the remaining oil and butter to the pan, reduce the heat to medium and cook the onions for 6–8 minutes until lightly golden. Stir in the carrots, garlic, thyme and tomato purée and cook for another 1–2 minutes, adding a splash of stock if needed.

Add any remaining seasoned flour followed by the ale and stir well. Add the stock, sugar, bay leaves and Worcestershire sauce. Bring to the boil, stirring, then return the beef, ensuring it is covered by liquid. Season well with salt and pepper. Part-cover and simmer for 1½ hours until the beef is just tender, adding a little more stock if needed. Check for seasoning and cook, uncovered, for 15–20 minutes until the sauce has reduced and thickened. Remove from the heat and leave to cool. Once cooled, stir in the mushrooms.

Roll out the pastry on a lightly floured work surface then put a 1.75-litre pie dish upside-down in the centre of it. Cut out a lid which is about 2.5cm larger all around than the dish. Cut off a thin strip from the edge of the remaining pastry, brush it with beaten egg and press it onto the rim of your pie dish.

Spoon the filling into the dish. Brush the strip of pastry with beaten egg and lay the pastry lid over the filling. Press the edges down firmly onto the top and underside of the rim to make a good seal, trim away any excess pastry and crimp around the edge with a fork (or use the tip of a piping nozzle for a pretty effect). Use a knife to cut a few small slits in the centre of the pie lid to allow steam to escape while cooking. Chill for 30 minutes if you have the time.

Preheat the oven to 200°C/180°C fan/gas 6. Brush the top of the pie with beaten egg and bake for 30–35 minutes until the top is golden and the filling is bubbling hot.

Mustard-Glazed Beef Kebabs & Baby Potato Skewers with Horseradish Dip

What's more appetising than a barbecued kebab? A kebab with the wonderful flavours of a traditional roast beef dinner! This is Sunday lunch, barbecue style – with beef sirloin marinated in mustard, honey and thyme served with rosemary baby potatoes and a horseradish dip. Fantastic! A great meal for al fresco dining but if the weather's not ideal you can cook it just as well on a griddle pan.

SERVES 4

750g beef sirloin
3 tbsp Dijon mustard
4 tbsp extra-virgin olive oil
2 tbsp runny honey
2 tbsp Worcestershire sauce
juice of ½ lemon
3 thyme sprigs, chopped
sea salt and freshly
    ground black pepper

For the potato skewers
16–20 baby new potatoes
1 tbsp runny honey
2 tbsp extra-virgin olive oil
1 tsp Dijon mustard
1 tsp chopped fresh
    rosemary leaves
3–4 large spring onions,
    trimmed and cut into
    3cm pieces

For the horseradish dip
150ml soured cream
1–2 tbsp freshly grated
    horseradish or
    horseradish sauce
1 tsp snipped chives

For the watercress salad
2 tbsp extra-virgin olive oil
a small bag (about 80g)
    of watercress
¼ red onion, thinly sliced
½ lemon, for squeezing

Trim the beef and cut into about 3cm cubes. Put the mustard, olive oil, honey, Worcestershire sauce, lemon juice, thyme and a little pinch each of salt and pepper in a shallow dish and mix well. Add the beef, tossing to coat and rubbing the marinade into the meat. Cover and leave to marinate in the fridge for at least 1 hour, preferably longer. Remove the beef from the fridge 30 minutes before cooking.

Meanwhile, put the potatoes in a large saucepan of salted cold water and bring to the boil. Cook for 14–16 minutes or until just tender, then drain well. Place the honey, olive oil, mustard and rosemary in a large bowl and mix well. Tip in the potatoes, season and toss to coat. Set aside.

In a small bowl, mix together the soured cream, horseradish and chives. Season with salt, cover and chill until needed.

Preheat a barbecue or griddle pan over a medium heat.

Shake off the excess marinade from the beef and thread onto skewers. Season with salt and pepper. Cook the skewers for 6–8 minutes, turning occasionally, depending on how you like your beef cooked. Once cooked, remove from the heat and allow to rest for a few minutes before serving.

Thread 4–5 baby potatoes onto each of 4 skewers, alternating with pieces of spring onion. Cook for 2–3 minutes on each side, basting with the marinade, until golden brown and slightly charred.

Drizzle the olive oil around the inside of a large bowl. Add the watercress and onion and gently swirl to coat the leaves in the oil. Add lemon juice to taste and season with salt and pepper.

Serve the beef and potato kebabs on a serving platter with the salad and horseradish dip.

Friday-Night Steak Fajitas

I've added coffee and cocoa to my steak marinade to punch up the Mexican mole flavour of these tasty fajitas. I've kept them quite mild, but feel free to add some cayenne or fresh chilli. A fantastic Friday-night meal (although great on any night!) for family and friends – quick and easy to cook and fun to share and eat. Dig in and enjoy!

SERVES 4

2–3 sirloin steaks
  (about 500g in total)
3 tbsp light olive
  or sunflower oil
1½ tsp instant espresso
  powder, dissolved in 25ml
  water (or 25ml extra
  strong espresso, cold)
2 tsp cacao powder
  or unsweetened
  cocoa powder
2 tsp ground ancho
  chilli powder or
  ancho chilli flakes
1 tsp chipotle chilli powder
  or sweet smoked paprika
1 tsp soft brown sugar
½ tsp ground cumin
½ tsp dried oregano
2 garlic cloves, minced
1 large onion, thinly sliced
3 peppers (a mixture
  of colours), de-seeded
  and sliced
8–10 baby plum or cherry
  tomatoes, halved
2 tbsp chopped coriander
  leaves, plus extra to serve
sea salt and freshly
  ground black pepper
8 medium soft corn
  or flour tortillas,
  warmed, to serve

For the zesty sour cream
150ml soured cream
1 lime, for squeezing,
  plus the zest of ½

Trim the steaks and cut into long strips. Put 1 tablespoon of the oil, espresso, cacao, ancho and chipotle chilli powders, sugar, cumin, oregano, half the garlic and a squeeze of lime juice into a bowl. Season well and mix together. Add the steak strips and toss to coat. Cover and leave to marinate for 30 minutes or longer if you have the time.

Mix the soured cream and lime zest together in a bowl. Add a little squeeze of lime juice to taste and season. Chill until needed.

Heat 1 tablespoon of the oil in a large, non-stick frying pan over a high heat and add the onion and peppers. Cook for 4 minutes, stirring, until softened and browned. Stir in the remaining garlic and cook for a few seconds until fragrant. Remove to a plate and set aside.

Add the remaining tablespoon of oil to the same pan and, when hot, add the steak slices. Cook for 2–3 minutes, stirring to prevent sticking. Return the onion and peppers to the pan and toss through the tomatoes to warm through for a minute (if preferred, you can keep the peppers and onions separate from the steak). Stir through the chopped coriander, squeeze over some lime juice and season with salt and pepper.

Arrange on a warm serving platter – or serve sizzling in the pan – sprinkled with coriander. Pile your tortillas with steak and the veg and add a drizzle of zesty soured cream. Fold up and enjoy!

Lamb Rogan Josh & Spring Onion Chapati

Rogan josh, with its intensely spiced creamy tomato sauce, is one of my favourite Indian curries. This dish takes a little time and effort but is easy to cook and definitely delivers on flavour. Curry night is always a good night in the Harriott house and I hope you enjoy this as much as we do.

SERVES 4

4 tbsp groundnut or sunflower oil
650g boneless lamb neck fillet or shoulder, trimmed and cut into 3cm cubes
3 cloves
2 bay leaves
4–5 cardamom pods, lightly crushed
1 small cinnamon stick
1 large onion, finely chopped
5cm piece of fresh root ginger, peeled and grated
4 garlic cloves, minced
2 tsp garam masala
1 tbsp ground coriander
1 tbsp ground cumin
2 tsp Kashmiri chilli powder (or mild chilli powder)
½–1 tsp cayenne, according to taste
½ tsp ground turmeric
1 tbsp tomato purée
200g Greek or natural yoghurt
1 x 227g tin chopped tomatoes
200ml chicken or lamb stock, hot, plus extra if needed
2 tbsp chopped coriander
sea salt and freshly ground black pepper

For the chapati
150g chapati flour (or 75g plain flour mixed with 75g fine wholemeal flour), plus extra for dusting
½ tsp salt
1 spring onion, trimmed and very finely sliced
100ml water
a little oil, for brushing

Add 2 tablespoons of the oil to a large deep-sided frying pan and, when hot, add the lamb and fry over a medium-high heat until lightly seared all over. Remove from the pan with a slotted spoon and set aside. Add the remaining oil and, when hot, add the cloves, bay leaves, cardamom and cinnamon to the pan and cook for 30 seconds until sizzling and fragrant. Add the onion and a pinch of salt. Cook over a medium heat for 8–10 minutes until softened and lightly browned. Add the ginger and garlic, 1 teaspoon of the garam masala and the rest of the ground spices and fry for 1–2 minutes. Return the meat to the pan along with any resting juices and stir in the tomato purée for 30 seconds. Add the yoghurt a tablespoon at a time, frying for about 20–30 seconds after each addition.

Stir in the tomatoes, stock, ½ teaspoon of salt and a good grind of black pepper. Cover and simmer gently for 45–50 minutes or until the lamb is tender, stirring occasionally and adding a little extra stock if needed. Remove the lid and cook for another 10–15 minutes so the sauce can reduce and thicken.

Meanwhile, make the chapati. Put the flour and salt into a large bowl and stir in the spring onion. Gradually add enough of the water, stirring with a wooden spoon, to make a fairly firm dough. Knead well for 5 minutes until soft and pliable (you can rub a little oil onto your fingers to help with kneading). Cover with a slightly damp tea towel and set aside to rest for 15 minutes.

Divide the dough into 4 equal balls, dust lightly with flour and roll out into roughly 16–18cm thin rounds. Heat a heavy-based non-stick frying pan or griddle over a medium-high heat and brush lightly with oil. When the pan is hot add the chapati one at a time and cook for 45–60 seconds on each side, or until a little puffy and brown, slightly charred patches appear. Put on a plate and keep warm while you cook the rest.

Stir the remaining garam masala and the coriander into the curry and serve in warmed bowls with basmati rice and the chapati.

Slow-Braised Lamb Shanks in Red Wine with Rosemary, Garlic & Anchovies

I'm definitely a lamb man and a slow-cooked lamb for Sunday lunch really is my good mood food! Lamb shanks are full of flavour and they taste fantastic when slow-cooked – they're perfect for a special treat. Anchovies with lamb is a wonderful flavour combination; the anchovies dissolve as the meat cooks, leaving behind a rich savoury seasoning. Don't be put off – it's not at all fishy!

SERVES 4

4 lamb shanks
2–3 tbsp light olive oil, plus an extra drizzle
1 tbsp butter (optional)
1 large onion, finely chopped
2 carrots, peeled and cut into thick slices
4–6 good-quality anchovy fillets in oil, drained and roughly chopped
4 garlic cloves, sliced
4 rosemary sprigs
2 tsp tomato purée
400ml red wine
450ml chicken or beef stock, plus extra if needed
zest and juice of ½ lemon
2 tbsp chopped flat-leaf parsley, plus extra to serve
freshly ground black pepper
creamy mash (page 216) or polenta (page 53), to serve

Preheat the oven to 180°C/160°C fan/gas 4.

Rub the lamb with a little drizzle of oil and season with pepper. Heat a large, heavy-based flameproof casserole over a medium heat, add 2 tablespoons of oil and, when hot, add the shanks. Fry on each side until lightly brown all over. (You may need to do one or two shanks at a time depending on the size of your shanks.) When they are all lightly browned, transfer to a plate. Add the butter (or a drizzle of oil), the onion and carrots to the casserole and cook for 6–8 minutes until softened and lightly golden. Stir in half the anchovies, the garlic and the rosemary for 30 seconds then stir in the tomato purée.

Add the wine and stir to release all the flavour from the bottom of the pan. Add the stock and return the shanks, pressing down to submerge as much as possible. Season with pepper and bring to a simmer. Cover and place in the oven for 2–2½ hours or until the meat is tender and just falling off the bone, turning the lamb halfway through and adding a little more stock if needed.

Remove the casserole from the oven and take out the shanks. Cover loosely with foil and rest for 10 minutes. Meanwhile, carefully pour the sauce from the casserole into a saucepan and put over a medium heat. Skim off any fat, if needed, and add the remaining anchovies, the lemon zest and a squeeze of juice to taste. Bring to a gentle boil for a few minutes until reduced by about a third. Stir in the parsley and check the seasoning.

To serve, spoon a large spoonful of mash or polenta into the centre of a serving bowl, sit a shank on top and spoon over some of the sauce. Scatter with parsley.

Sumac Lamb Kofta with Coriander Flatbreads

Subtly spiced with wonderful Levantine flavours, these coriander flatbreads topped with lamb kebabs and tangy sumac onions are a real tasty treat. This really is the kind of food that makes me happy.

SERVES 4

2 tsp cumin seeds
500g minced lamb
2 garlic cloves, minced
1 tbsp finely chopped
    parsley, plus extra
    leaves to serve
1 tbsp finely chopped mint,
    plus extra leaves to serve
1½ tsp ground sumac
1 tsp ground allspice
½ tsp ground coriander
1 tsp pul biber or ½ tsp
    chilli flakes
oil, for spraying or drizzling
sea salt and freshly
    ground black pepper

For the sumac onions
1 small red onion, peeled
    and thinly sliced
¾ tsp sumac
1 tbsp finely chopped
    flat-leaf parsley
1 tbsp extra-virgin olive oil
½ lemon, for squeezing

For the chilli-mint yoghurt
150ml natural yoghurt
1 tsp dried mint
1 green chilli, de-seeded
    and finely chopped

For the flatbreads
250g plain flour, plus
    extra for dusting
2 tsp baking powder
1 heaped tsp coriander
    seeds, toasted and ground
¾ tsp salt
250g thick Greek yoghurt

To serve
hummus
sliced tomato
sliced cucumber
pomegranate seeds

First, make the sumac onions. Put the onion in a sieve and slowly pour over a full kettle of boiling water. Drain and leave to cool. Pat dry and put into a small bowl. Sprinkle over the sumac and a good pinch of sea salt. Mix well to combine and stir in the parsley, olive oil and a squeeze of lemon juice. Chill until needed.

For the chilli-mint yoghurt, in a small bowl mix together the yoghurt, dried mint and chilli. Stir in a little lemon juice and season to taste with salt. Chill until needed.

To make the flatbreads, mix the flour, baking powder, coriander and salt in a large bowl. Make a well in the centre, pour in the yoghurt and bring the flour into the centre. Mix together into a soft dough – if too dry, add a splash of water. Tip the dough onto a lightly floured work surface and knead briefly. Place the dough in a lightly oiled bowl, cover and rest for 15 minutes.

Once the dough has rested, portion the dough into 4 equal pieces. Using a floured rolling pin, roll each piece of dough into a round 20–25cm in diameter and about 3mm thick. Heat a frying pan over a medium heat. Cook each flatbread for 1–2 minutes on each side until nicely puffed. Keep warm.

Toast the cumin seeds in a dry frying pan over a medium heat until fragrant. Tip into a pestle and mortar and crush, then place in a large bowl. Add the lamb, garlic, herbs and spices, and season generously with salt and pepper. Mix and squeeze together with your hands to ensure that everything is well combined. With slightly damp hands, mould the meat mixture into sausage shapes around 4 flat skewers. Flatten them slightly, making little indents, until they are around 2.5cm in thickness.

Preheat a barbecue or chargrill pan to medium-high. Drizzle or spray the kofta skewers with a little oil. Cook for 6–8 minutes, turning occasionally, or until cooked to your liking.

To serve, spread some hummus onto a flatbread, add tomato and cucumber slices, slide the kebabs from the skewers and place on top. Scatter with sumac onions, plenty of fresh herb leaves, pomegranate seeds and a drizzle of chilli-mint yoghurt.

One-Pot Baked Lamb Orzo with Spinach, Black Olives & Feta

Bring the warm flavours of the Mediterranean to your table with this fantastic one-pot dish full of aromatic Greek herbs and spices. Orzo looks like a large grain of rice but it's actually a pasta and it has a wonderful velvety texture that's perfect for a comforting family meal. A super easy, flavour-packed meal with very little washing up is most definitely what I call good mood food.

SERVES 4

500g lamb rump steaks, trimmed of fat and cut into chunks
2 tbsp olive oil, plus extra for drizzling
½ lemon, for squeezing
1½ tsp ground allspice
1 tsp dried oregano
2 garlic cloves, finely chopped
1 large onion, chopped
1 small cinnamon stick
2 tsp tomato purée
½ tsp chilli flakes
1 x 400g tin cherry tomatoes
1 tbsp runny honey
a large rosemary sprig
550ml chicken stock
250g orzo
100g baby spinach leaves
60g black olives, pitted and halved
80g feta, crumbled
2 tbsp chopped flat-leaf parsley
sea salt and freshly ground black pepper

Place the lamb in a large bowl with a good drizzle of olive oil, a squeeze of lemon juice, 1 teaspoon of the allspice, ½ teaspoon of the oregano and half the garlic. Season with salt and pepper and mix well. Cover and leave to marinate for at least 30 minutes, preferably longer.

Preheat the oven to 200°C/180°C fan/gas 6.

Heat the oil in a large flameproof casserole over a medium-high heat and add the lamb. Cook for 3–4 minutes to sear the meat. Remove from the pan with a slotted spoon and set aside.

In the same pan, add the onion, lower the heat to medium and cook for 4–6 minutes until softened but not coloured. Add the cinnamon, remaining garlic, allspice and oregano and cook for 30 seconds until fragrant. Add the tomato purée and chilli flakes and stir before adding the tomatoes, honey, rosemary and stock. Season with a little salt and a generous grind of pepper. Return the lamb to the pan, bring to the boil, then reduce the heat, cover and gently simmer for 5 minutes.

Add the orzo and give everything a good stir. Transfer the casserole, uncovered, to the oven. Bake for 20–25 minutes until the orzo is tender but still with bite.

Remove from the oven, take out the cinnamon stick and stir through the spinach. Cover and allow to rest for 5 minutes before stirring in the olives. Serve scattered with the feta and chopped parsley.

Honey & Chilli-Spiked Lamb with Potato, Bean & Mint Dressing Salad

This is a delightful warm salad twist on a traditional lamb and mint sauce. It's fantastic for a summery Sunday lunch and also great for barbecues. This is also an easy salad to adapt and make with leftover roast lamb.

SERVES 4

3 tbsp olive oil
1 garlic clove, minced
1½ tbsp runny honey
½ tsp chilli flakes
1 tsp dried mint
3–4 lamb leg steaks
    (600–700g in total),
    trimmed
sea salt and freshly
    ground black pepper

For the salad
650g salad potatoes,
    halved or quartered
200g green beans, trimmed
olive oil, for cooking
a pinch of chilli flakes
a drizzle of honey
a small bag (about 60g)
    of mixed baby spinach
    and rocket
a handful of mint leaves,
    shredded
a handful of flat-leaf
    parsley, leaves torn
80g feta (optional)
1 medium-hot red chilli,
    de-seeded and thinly
    sliced into rings

For the mint dressing
2 tsp demerara or
    white sugar
2 tbsp red wine vinegar
a pinch of chilli flakes
3–4 tbsp extra-virgin
    olive oil
a small bunch of mint
    (about 15g), leaves picked
    and very finely chopped

To make the dressing, put the sugar and vinegar in a small bowl and stir to dissolve the sugar. Add the chilli flakes and whisk in the extra-virgin olive oil. Stir in the mint, season with a little salt and set aside.

Meanwhile, in a large shallow dish, mix together the olive oil, garlic, honey, chilli flakes and dried mint. Add the lamb steaks, season with salt and pepper and mix well to coat. Cover and set aside to marinate for 20 minutes or so while you cook the potatoes (or cover and chill to marinate for longer if you have the time).

Place the potatoes in a saucepan of salted water and bring to the boil over a medium-high heat. Cook for 12–14 minutes or until tender. Drain and set aside. Add the green beans to a small saucepan of salted boiling water and boil for 3–5 minutes until tender. Drain and refresh in cold water. Drain again and set aside.

Put a chargrill pan or large frying pan over a medium-high heat. Shake any excess marinade from the steaks and cook for 3–4 minutes on each side (depending on thickness and how you like your lamb cooked). Remove from the pan, cover loosely with foil to keep warm and rest for 6–8 minutes.

Add a drizzle of olive oil to the same pan and add the potatoes, chilli flakes, a drizzle of honey and season lightly with salt and pepper. Fry over a medium-high heat for 3–4 minutes until lightly golden. Add the beans and toss through to coat. Remove from the heat to cool a little.

Put the warm potatoes and beans in a large bowl and add the salad leaves. Drizzle over a little of the mint dressing and toss together. Slice the rested lamb into 1cm slices.

Tip the potatoes and salad onto a serving platter and scatter with the herbs. Arrange the lamb slices on top. Crumble over the feta (if using), scatter over the chilli slices and drizzle over the remaining dressing. Serve immediately.

Gochujang & Ginger Stir-Fried Pork & Greens

Once you've tried this super-tasty Korean-inspired chilli pork with crunchy greens you'll think twice about ordering a takeaway! Gochujang has quite a kick so adjust according to taste or, if you prefer, you can swap for a sriracha or sweet chilli sauce – although it's really worth trying the Korean spice paste for its complex savoury and sweet spice. Feel free to mix up the veggies to use whatever's in season and serve with some steamed rice.

SERVES 4

3 tbsp rice wine, mirin or dry sherry
3 tbsp low-sodium soy sauce
500g pork loin or fillet, thinly sliced
2 tsp cornflour
1 garlic clove, minced
1 tbsp sesame oil
2 tbsp Gochujang paste
1 tbsp honey
1 tbsp hot water
3 tbsp groundnut or sunflower oil
5cm piece of fresh root ginger, peeled and cut into thin matchsticks
1 medium-hot red chilli, de-seeded and sliced (optional)
3 spring onions, trimmed and cut into 2cm pieces
1 large courgette, trimmed and cut on the diagonal into 5mm slices
125g mangetout or sugar snap peas
200g spring greens, chard or cavolo nero, stems and ribs removed, thinly shredded
sea salt and freshly ground black pepper

To finish
2 tsp sesame seeds, toasted
1 spring onion, trimmed and shredded

Mix 1 tablespoon of the rice wine, 1 tablespoon of the soy sauce and 1 tablespoon of cold water in a shallow dish and add the pork slices. Toss to coat, mixing well until most of the liquid has been absorbed. Add the cornflour, garlic, a good grind of pepper and 2 teaspoons of the sesame oil, and mix again. Cover and leave to marinate for 20 minutes.

In a small bowl, mix together the remaining rice wine, soy sauce, the Gochujang paste, honey and hot water. Mix together until well combined, then set aside.

Heat a wok over a high heat and, when it is lightly smoking, add 2 tablespoons of the groundnut oil. When hot, add the pork, stir-frying for 2–3 minutes until seared and lightly golden. Remove with a slotted spoon and transfer to a plate.

Add the remaining groundnut oil to the wok and stir-fry the ginger, chilli (if using) and spring onions for 30 seconds. Add all the vegetables and stir-fry for 2–3 minutes until they begin to wilt, then add the Gochujang mixture and cook, stirring, for 30 seconds until aromatic.

Return the pork to the wok. Stir-fry for a final minute or two until the sauce has coated everything and the pork is cooked through. Remove from the heat and stir in the remaining sesame oil.

Finish sprinkled with sesame seeds and shredded spring onion.

Pan-Fried Pork Loin Steaks with Swede Mash & Cider-Mustard Sauce

Pork and apple is a classic flavour combination and my cider and mustard sauce is a quick and delicious accompaniment that's both vibrant and comforting. Swede makes a lovely bittersweet mash that pairs perfectly with the creamy and tangy sauce. I'm using pork loin steaks but you can use pork chops or tenderloin – just adjust the meat cooking times accordingly. Serve with your favourite green vegetables.

SERVES 4

4 boneless thick-cut
 pork loin steaks,
 at room temperature
1 tbsp light olive oil,
 plus an extra drizzle
2 banana shallots,
 finely chopped
1 tsp fresh thyme leaves
250ml dry cider
150ml double cream
zest of 1 lemon
1½ tbsp grain mustard
2 tbsp chopped
 flat-leaf parsley
sea salt and freshly
 ground black pepper

For the swede mash
1 large swede, peeled and
 cut into 2.5cm chunks
1–2 tbsp butter
a pinch of ground nutmeg
sea salt and ground
 white pepper

Put the swede in a large, lidded saucepan and cover with cold water. Add ½ teaspoon salt and bring to the boil. Reduce the heat and simmer for 15–20 minutes or until tender, stirring occasionally. Drain well and allow to steam dry in the colander for a few minutes. Return to the pan and mash until smooth. Season with salt and white pepper and set aside.

Pat the pork steaks dry and season well on both sides with salt and pepper.

Heat the oil in a large heavy-based frying pan over a medium-high heat and sear the pork for 1–2 minutes. Turn and sear the other side for 1–2 minutes, then reduce the heat to medium and continue to cook for a further 4–6 minutes (not forgetting the fat edge) or until browned and just cooked through. Remove from the pan and set aside.

Add a drizzle of oil to the pan, if needed, and cook the shallots and thyme for 2–3 minutes until softened and starting to colour. Add the cider, bring to the boil and reduce by half. Stir through the cream and bring to the boil to thicken. Reduce the heat, stir in the lemon zest, mustard and half the parsley. Season to taste with salt and pepper.

Return the pork and its juices to the pan and cook gently for 1–2 minutes or until the pork is hot and fully cooked through. Check for seasoning.

Meanwhile, return the swede mash to the heat to warm through, and stir through the butter and nutmeg. Check for seasoning.

Serve the pork and mash with the sauce, garnished with the remaining parsley and a side of green veg.

Easy Sausage, Bacon & Bean Bake

Sometimes simplicity is best and that's definitely the case with this satisfying bake made mostly with store-cupboard ingredients – it's perfect for busy days and is sure to please the entire family. I like to use Italian sausages which are full of flavour and slightly sweet and aromatic with fennel. They work perfectly with the mild beans in this bake, but feel free to use any sausages you like – or leave out the bacon and use vegetarian sausages for a simple and tasty veggie meal.

SERVES 4

2 tbsp light olive oil
6–8 good-quality sausages
4 streaky bacon rashers,
    roughly chopped
1 large onion, sliced
2 garlic cloves, minced
½ tsp dried mixed herbs
200ml chicken or
    vegetable stock
1 x 400g tin chopped
    tomatoes
1 tbsp tomato ketchup
½ tbsp balsamic vinegar
    or balsamic glaze
1 x 400g tin butter beans,
    drained and rinsed
1 x 400g tin cannellini
    beans, drained
    and rinsed
2 tbsp chopped flat-leaf
    parsley, plus extra
    to serve
a pinch of sugar (optional)
sea salt and freshly
    ground black pepper

Preheat the oven to 180°C/160°C fan/gas 4.

In an ovenproof sauté pan or shallow flameproof casserole, heat 1 tablespoon of the oil over a medium heat and add the sausages. Cook for 4–5 minutes or until sealed and lightly browned on all sides. Transfer to a plate and set aside.

Add the bacon to the pan and fry until brown all over. Add the remaining oil then add the onion. Cook for 4–6 minutes until softened. Add the garlic and dried herbs and cook for 30 seconds until fragrant. Add the stock to deglaze the pan then stir in the tomatoes, ketchup, balsamic vinegar and all the beans. Bring to a simmer, stir in the parsley and season to taste (add a little sugar to sweeten the tomato if needed).

Nestle the sausages among the beans and bake in the oven for 20–25 minutes or until the beans are bubbling and the sausages are cooked through. Serve straight to the table sprinkled with parsley, with some fresh crusty bread on the side.

Creole Jambalaya

Jambalaya is a rice dish that's full of smoky, spicy flavours, and this is an easy stove-top version that doesn't take too much time or effort. The aromatic sofrito-like trinity of onion, celery and peppers is the basis of Cajun and Creole cooking and this is sautéed before adding layers of flavour to this satisfying meal that the whole family will enjoy. If you want a fancier looking dish, use raw jumbo tiger prawns and fry them separately with a squeeze of lemon and a pinch of paprika, and serve on top of the finished dish.

SERVES 4–6

1–2 tbsp light olive
   or sunflower oil
125g smoked spicy sausage
   (Andouille/chorizo/
   merguez), sliced
6 skinless and boneless
   chicken thighs, quartered
1 large onion, finely
   chopped
2 peppers (red and/or green),
   de-seeded and diced
2 celery sticks, trimmed
   and finely chopped
4 spring onions, trimmed
   and sliced, whites and
   greens separated
3 garlic cloves, minced
1 tsp dried oregano
1 tsp fresh thyme leaves
1 tsp sweet smoked paprika
½ tsp cayenne (more if you
   like it spicy)
300g long-grain rice
2 tsp tomato purée
1 x 227g tin chopped
   tomatoes
600ml chicken or
   vegetable stock
150g medium raw or cooked
   prawns, peeled and
   deveined if necessary,
   from a sustainable source
a handful of baby plum or
   cherry tomatoes, halved
3 tbsp chopped flat-leaf
   parsley, plus extra
   to serve
sea salt and freshly
   ground black pepper
Tabasco (optional), to serve

Heat 1 tablespoon of oil in a flameproof casserole or heavy-based saucepan that has a lid and add the sausage slices. Cook for 1–2 minutes until lightly browned. Remove from the pan with a slotted spoon and set aside. Add the chicken and cook over a medium-high heat for 4–6 minutes until golden on all sides. Remove with a slotted spoon and set aside.

If needed, add another tablespoon of oil to the pan, then cook the onion, peppers and celery for 4–6 minutes over a medium heat until softened but not coloured. Add the spring onion whites and the garlic and cook for 30 seconds. Add the oregano, thyme and spices and cook for 1 minute until fragrant. Stir in the rice until well coated in the spices then stir in the tomato purée and add the tinned tomatoes. Add the stock, stir and return the chicken, sausage and any resting juices to the pan. Season and bring to the boil. Cover with a tight-fitting lid, reduce the heat and simmer for 18–20 minutes, or until the chicken is cooked through. Fold through the prawns 2 minutes before the end of cooking time.

Remove the lid, stir in the fresh tomatoes and parsley. Replace the lid, ensuring it's on tightly, remove from the heat and allow to rest for 8–10 minutes.

Serve in warmed bowls, scattered with the spring onion greens and some extra parsley. Add a dash of Tabasco if you like a bit more heat.

Fiery BBQ Glazed Pork Ribs with Mango, Black Bean & Rice Salad

Sticky, tender and crispy ribs are perfect for a summer barbecue and when cooked well can really bring a smile to your face... quite literally if you eat them like I do! This is my Caribbean twist on a barbecue sauce – with a 'ikkle bit of fruity rum and spice.

SERVES 4–6

1.5kg baby back pork ribs, cut into racks of 3–4 ribs
1 onion, peeled and quartered
2 star anise
4 garlic cloves, peeled
6–8 whole allspice (pimento) berries
sea salt and freshly ground black pepper

For the BBQ sauce
6 tbsp tomato ketchup
5 tbsp dark brown sugar
3 tbsp runny honey
3 tbsp dark rum
2 tbsp soy sauce
1 tbsp Worcestershire sauce
½–1 Scotch bonnet chilli, de-seeded and chopped
2 garlic cloves, minced
½ tsp ground nutmeg
zest and juice of ½ lime
juice of ½ orange
2 tsp English mustard

For the rice salad
1–2 x 250g packs ready-cooked basmati rice
1 tbsp desiccated coconut
1 large mango, peeled, stoned and diced
1 x 227g tin black beans, drained and rinsed
a handful of coriander leaves, roughly chopped
2 spring onions, trimmed and thinly sliced
zest and juice of ½ lime
1 tsp runny honey
2–3 tbsp olive oil
hot pepper sauce, to taste

Put the ribs into one large saucepan if you can, or divide between two. Add the onion, star anise, garlic, allspice and 2 teaspoons of salt, and cover with water. Bring to a rolling boil, reduce the heat and simmer for 40–50 minutes until tender but not falling apart.

Meanwhile, put all the ingredients for the BBQ sauce into a saucepan over a medium heat and bring to the boil for a minute or two. Reduce the heat and gently simmer for 4–6 minutes. Taste, season and adjust for sweetness and acidity with honey and lime juice. Remove from the heat and allow to cool completely.

Heat the rice according to the packet instructions. Empty out into a wide, shallow dish to speed up the cooling process, and fluff with a fork to separate the grains. Set aside.

Remove the ribs from the heat and carefully drain. Pat them dry and place in a large dish or tray. Baste well on all sides with the BBQ sauce and leave to marinate while you prepare the salad.

In a dry frying pan over a medium heat, gently toast the desiccated coconut until lightly golden; keep an eye on it because it can easily burn. Remove from the heat and set aside.

Put the cooled rice in a serving bowl and add the toasted coconut, diced mango, beans, coriander and spring onions. Toss together. Whisk together the lime zest and juice, honey and oil and season with hot sauce to taste, salt and pepper. When ready to serve, drizzle some dressing over the rice salad and toss together to coat.

Preheat a barbecue or griddle pan to medium.

Season the ribs with a little salt and cook on a barbecue or lightly oiled griddle pan for 10–12 minutes until caramelised and slightly charred, basting with more BBQ sauce as they cook. (Alternatively, roast in a 200°C/180°C fan/gas 6 oven for 15–20 minutes, basting often.) Serve with the rice salad on the side.

Chapter Five

DESSERTS & SWEET TREATS

Fresh Fruit, Cucumber & Soft Herb Salad with Pimm's Granita

Think of a British summer and you think of… rain… well ok, think again… Pimm's! With a combination of Pimm's, strawberries, cucumber and mint, this refreshing dessert is sunshine and happiness in a bowl and it makes a delightful end to a meal or a fruity treat on a warm afternoon. The granita needs to be made ahead to give it time to freeze. The fruit salad can be served with ice cream or a fruity sorbet for the kids.

SERVES 6

400g strawberries,
  halved or quartered
½ cucumber, halved
  lengthways and sliced
2 oranges, peeled and pith
  removed, segmented
2 ripe nectarines,
  stoned and sliced
6–8 large basil leaves,
  shredded
a handful of mint leaves,
  shredded, plus extra
  to decorate
zest and juice of
  ½ large lemon
1 tbsp honey or maple syrup
a pinch of flaky salt (pink
  Himalayan if you have it)

For the Pimm's granita
150g caster sugar
500ml water
1 large mint sprig
zest and juice of
  1 large lemon
175ml Pimm's

First, make the granita. Put the sugar and water into a saucepan over a medium heat and stir until the sugar has dissolved. Bring to the boil then add the mint sprig, reduce the heat and simmer gently for 6–8 minutes. Remove from the heat and leave to cool completely before removing the mint and stirring in the lemon zest and juice, and the Pimm's.

Pour the liquid into a wide, shallow, freezer-proof container. Place in the freezer for 2½–3 hours, after which time ice crystals should have formed. Fork through the granita to break up the ice crystals, then place back in the freezer. Repeat the process 2 or 3 times every 1–2 hours until the granita is completely frozen, with a light and fluffy texture.

When the granita is ready, put all the prepared fruit in a large bowl with the shredded herbs. Toss to combine. In a small bowl, whisk together the lemon zest and juice, and honey. Pour over the fruit and gently toss to combine. Cover and chill in the fridge for 15 minutes before serving. Add a pinch of flaky salt and gently toss.

Serve the fruit salad in dessert glasses with a scoop or two of granita. Decorate with mint leaves.

Baked Vanilla & Ginger Custard with Stem Ginger Rhubarb

This is an old-fashioned, comforting baked custard with a twist. Stem ginger syrup adds a gentle sweet spice to the creamy custard and it works perfectly with tart rhubarb and ginger. You really can't beat the winning combination of rhubarb and custard and it brings back so many joyful childhood memories. If you prefer a punchier ginger flavour or you don't have a jar of stem ginger, you can add a tablespoon of finely grated fresh ginger to the custard and rhubarb. The baked custard is also delicious with poached plums or peaches.

SERVES 6

3 large eggs
1 egg yolk
50g caster sugar
1 tsp vanilla extract
250ml milk
200ml double cream
zest of ½ orange
2–3 tbsp syrup from
    a jar of stem ginger
½ tsp ground ginger

For the stem ginger rhubarb
500g rhubarb, cut
    into 4cm lengths
2 pieces of stem ginger,
    thinly sliced
1 star anise (optional)
zest and juice of
    1 large orange
80g light brown
    or caster sugar

Preheat the oven to 170°C/150°C fan/gas 3.

In a large bowl, lightly whisk together the eggs, egg yolk, sugar and vanilla extract.

Put the milk, cream and orange zest in a saucepan over a low-medium heat and heat, stirring, to just below boiling point. Stir in the stem ginger syrup. Remove from the heat and slowly whisk into the eggs in the bowl. Pour into a 1-litre baking dish (strain through a sieve if you want to remove the zest).

Stand the baking dish in a deep roasting tin and pour hot water into the tin until it comes halfway up the baking dish. Sift the ground ginger over the top of the custard. Bake for 40–45 minutes until set but with a slight wobble.

Meanwhile, put the rhubarb, stem ginger, star anise (if using), orange zest and juice, sugar and 2 tbsp water into a saucepan over a medium heat. Cover and bring to the boil. Reduce the heat and gently simmer for 5–7 minutes depending on the thickness of the rhubarb, stirring occasionally, until the sugar has dissolved, the liquid is syrupy and the rhubarb is cooked but still holding its shape.

Serve warm or chilled.

A Wonderful Wandsworth Mess

I'm a Wandsworth boy with Caribbean roots, and this is my twist on the summer classic, Eton mess. The tropical flavours of mango, passion fruit and lime really lift this easy and quick-to-prepare English dessert to another level. I've added a splash of coconut rum which I think works perfectly, but you can stick with a squeeze of lime if you prefer.

SERVES 4

2 large mangos, peeled, stoned and diced, a few pieces reserved to decorate
3 passion fruit
1 tbsp shredded mint leaves, plus extra sprigs to decorate
zest and juice of ½ lime
2 tbsp coconut rum (optional)
300ml double cream
2 tsp icing sugar
4–5 shop-bought meringue nests (depending on size), broken into bite-sized pieces
edible flowers, to decorate (optional)

Put the diced mango and the pulp from ½ passion fruit in a bowl with the shredded mint and lime zest. Stir in the coconut rum (if using) and add a little lime juice to taste. Set aside.

In a large bowl, whisk the cream with the icing sugar until it just starts to hold soft peaks. Fold through the crushed meringues (reserving a few pieces for decoration) then swirl through the pulp from 1½ passion fruit.

Put a layer of macerated mango in the bottom of 4 chilled dessert glasses. Add some of the meringue cream, top with more macerated mango and finish with another layer of meringue cream. Drizzle over the remaining passion fruit pulp. Decorate with a few pieces of fresh mango, the reserved meringue pieces, mint sprigs and edible flowers (if using).

Carrot, Orange & Rosemary Loaf Cake

Baking is surely one of the most pleasing and satisfying forms of cooking. Just the smell of a cake baking can quickly lift your mood. Carrot cake is a classic British favourite and a cake that works for all occasions – whether it's for a celebration or just for an afternoon pick-me-up. This moist carrot loaf cake is incredibly easy to make and tastes wonderful with the subtle hint of orange and rosemary. Enjoy!

MAKES 10–12 SLICES

200ml vegetable oil,
    plus extra for greasing
250g plain flour
1 tsp baking powder
½ tsp salt
1½ tsp ground cinnamon
100g caster sugar
100g soft light brown sugar
1 tsp vanilla extract
zest and juice of 1 orange,
    plus extra zest to decorate
3 large eggs
200g grated peeled carrots
2 tbsp finely chopped
    rosemary, plus a few
    small sprigs to decorate

*For the cream
    cheese topping*
125g cream cheese,
    at room temperature
25g butter, softened
25g icing sugar

Preheat the oven to 180°C/160°C fan/gas 4. Grease a 900g/2lb loaf tin and line with baking parchment.

In a large bowl, mix the flour, baking powder, salt and cinnamon.

In a separate bowl, whisk together the oil, both sugars, vanilla, orange zest and juice, and eggs until well combined. Make a well in the flour ingredients and pour in the liquid. Stir until you have a smooth batter. Fold in the grated carrots and chopped rosemary.

Transfer the mixture to the prepared tin and smooth the surface with the back of a spoon. Bake for 1–1¼ hours until the cake has risen and is golden and springy to the touch. Insert a skewer into the centre and check it comes out clean.

Meanwhile, make the topping. Using an electric hand-held mixer on a medium speed, beat the cream cheese, butter and icing sugar together until creamy. Cover and chill until ready to use.

Leave the cake to cool in the tin for 15 minutes before turning out onto a wire rack to cool completely. Spread the cream cheese topping over the top of the cooled cake and decorate with orange zest and rosemary sprigs.

Chocolate Sponge Traybake with Salted Caramel Sauce

This delightful chocolate sponge traybake is a throwback to my childhood. I loved chocolate sponge pudding at school and so years later I often recreated it at home for my kids. I've added chocolate chips and a few bittersweet cacao nibs to add a bit of a modern twist and texture to this super-easy traybake, and the salted caramel sauce adds a little bit of grown-up indulgence.

SERVES 9

250g butter, softened, plus extra for greasing
125g caster sugar
125g soft light brown sugar
4 medium eggs
200g self-raising flour
2 tsp baking powder
50g good-quality cocoa powder
a pinch of salt
3 tbsp milk
100g dark chocolate chips
1 tsp cacao nibs (optional)
vanilla ice cream, to serve

For the salted caramel sauce
150g soft light brown sugar
2 tbsp golden syrup
250ml double cream
50g butter
½ tsp flaky sea salt

Preheat the oven to 180°C/160°C fan/gas 4. Grease a deep-sided baking tin, 20 x 25cm, and line with baking parchment.

In a large bowl and using an electric hand-held mixer, beat the butter and both sugars together until light and fluffy. Gradually add the eggs, beating well after each addition. Sift over the flour, baking powder, cocoa and salt. Beat until well combined then add the milk and stir. Fold in the chocolate chips.

Pour into the prepared baking tin and level out the top with the back of a spoon or a spatula. Sprinkle over the cacao nibs (if using). Bake for 40 minutes or until a skewer inserted into the centre comes out clean. Leave to cool slightly in the tin.

To make the caramel sauce, place all the ingredients in a small saucepan over a low to medium heat. Gently bring to the boil, stirring until the sugar has dissolved. Boil for 2 minutes, remove from the heat and leave to stand for 5 minutes before serving.

Cut the sponge into 9 squares and serve with the caramel sauce and a scoop of vanilla ice cream.

White Chocolate, Macadamia & Raspberry Blondies

Blondies are often referred to as blonde brownies and, although they don't contain cocoa, they are just as delicious as the more traditional brownie. These blondies are an easy bake, and the combination of buttery macadamia nuts and creamy white chocolate is fabulous. I've topped them with freeze-dried raspberries for an intense burst of fruitiness and colour.

MAKES 12

250g butter, melted, plus extra for greasing
3 large eggs
250g caster sugar
175g plain flour
20g white chocolate chips
150g macadamia nuts, chopped
100g white chocolate, melted
1 tbsp freeze-dried raspberries

Preheat the oven to 180°C/160°C fan/gas 4. Grease a 20 x 28cm baking tin and line with baking parchment.

In a bowl and using an electric hand-held whisk, beat the eggs and sugar until the mixture is pale and mousse-like and has doubled in size (when you lift the whisk out of the mixture it should leave a trail for a couple of seconds before disappearing).

Add the melted butter a little at a time while whisking, making sure each addition is fully mixed in before adding the next.

Sift in the flour and fold the mixture together. Add the chocolate chips and 100g of the macadamia nuts and gently fold again. Pour the mixture into the prepared tin and bake in the oven for 35–40 minutes or until just cooked through and a skewer inserted into the centre comes out clean. Leave to cool completely in the tin.

Gently remove from the tin (use the baking parchment to lift it out), drizzle over the melted white chocolate and sprinkle over the remaining chopped macadamias and the freeze-dried raspberries. Allow the chocolate to set before cutting into 12 portions.

Pistachio, Polenta & Lemon Cakes

These delectable gluten-free cakes are wonderfully nutty with pistachios and almonds and tangy from the citrus syrup and icing. They're moist, sticky and yummy – just perfect for an afternoon treat. I'm not using any baking powder in the recipe so it's important to beat everything well.

MAKES 9–12

200g butter, softened,
   plus extra for greasing
100g shelled unsalted
   pistachios
200g golden caster sugar
3 large eggs
50g ground almonds
100g fine polenta
zest and juice of ½ lemon

For the lemon syrup
40g sugar
zest and juice of 2½ lemons

To decorate
10 tbsp icing sugar
zest and juice of 1 lemon
2 tbsp shelled unsalted
   pistachios, half finely
   ground and half
   roughly chopped

Preheat the oven to 180°C/160°C fan/gas 4. Grease 9 rectangular cake moulds or mini loaf tins and line with baking parchment. (Alternatively, grease and line a 12-hole cake tin.)

Place the pistachios in a food processor and blitz until finely and evenly ground.

In a large mixing bowl and using an electric hand-held mixer, beat the butter and sugar together until pale. Scrape the sides of the bowl and beat well again. Add the eggs, one at a time, continuing to beat really well after each addition. Fold in the ground pistachios and the ground almonds. Add the polenta, and the lemon zest and juice. Mix gently until combined.

Divide the mixture evenly between the prepared moulds. Place on a baking tray and bake for 20–25 minutes or until a skewer inserted into the centre of one comes out clean.

Meanwhile, make the lemon syrup. In a small saucepan, heat the sugar with the lemon zest and juice. Bring to the boil and stir until the sugar has melted. Remove from the heat to cool a little.

Prick small holes in the top of the cooked cakes with a skewer and pour 1–2 teaspoons of the warm (make sure it's not hot) syrup over each cake. Leave to cool for 15–20 minutes to allow the syrup to soak in.

In a bowl, mix the icing sugar with enough lemon juice to make a thick but runny icing. When the cakes have cooled, remove them from the moulds and spoon or drizzle over the icing. Decorate with a sprinkling of ground and chopped pistachios and the lemon zest.

Blueberry & Almond Clafoutis with Cardamom Cream

A traditional French clafoutis is made with cherries but I love the unique, perfumed sweet sourness of blueberries, and they go so well with almond. The ground almonds make this slightly less custard-like than a typical clafoutis. Instead, it has more texture and flavour, like a deliciously light cake batter. Serving with a cardamom cream may sound peculiar, yet the combination of the citrusy, aromatic spice with the vanilla notes in the sweet berries really does work. I like to call this bluefoutis, but maybe that's just me!

SERVES 4–6

a small knob of butter,
   for greasing
100g caster sugar, plus
   extra for sprinkling
250g fresh blueberries
zest of 1 lemon
125ml whole milk
150ml double cream
½ tsp almond extract
   or 1 tsp vanilla extract
3 large eggs
30g plain flour
40g ground almonds
1 tsp baking powder
a pinch of salt

For the cardamom cream
250ml double cream
1 tbsp icing sugar,
   plus extra for dusting
seeds of 4–5 cardamon
   pods, crushed

Preheat the oven to 180°C/160°C fan/gas 4.

Grease a 20cm ovenproof baking or pie dish with the butter and sprinkle with 2 tablespoons of caster sugar to coat the inside. Put the blueberries in the bottom of the dish and scatter over the lemon zest.

Mix together the milk, cream and almond extract.

In a separate mixing bowl, whisk the eggs and sugar together until light and frothy, then stir in the flour, ground almonds, baking powder and salt. Gradually pour the milk mixture onto the eggs, whisking all the time, until the batter is smooth and creamy, but being careful not to overmix.

Pour the batter over the blueberries and sprinkle with caster sugar. Bake in the oven for 35–40 minutes or until puffy, golden and just set with a slight wobble in the middle.

Meanwhile, whisk the double cream and icing sugar together until soft peaks form. Fold in the cardamon until well combined. Chill until needed.

Remove the clafoutis from the oven and transfer the dish to a wire rack for 5–10 minutes. The clafoutis will deflate a little as it cools, but don't worry! Dust with icing sugar and serve warm or at room temperature, topped with a spoonful of the cardamom cream.

Rich Chocolate & Espresso Cheescake

Well, you can't get a better boost to your mood than this fabulously rich and indulgent cheesecake. It's a simple-to-make chocolate cheesecake with a subtle hint of espresso – a perfect dessert for a dinner party or special treat.

SERVES 8–10

200g good-quality dark chocolate (minimum 70% cocoa solids), chopped
250g full-fat cream cheese, at room temperature
3 tbsp icing sugar
1 tsp vanilla extract
1 tbsp good-quality cocoa powder
220ml double cream, at room temperature

For the base
80g butter, plus extra for greasing
200g dark chocolate digestive biscuits
2 tsp caster sugar
2 tsp instant espresso powder

For the ganache topping
100g good-quality dark chocolate (minimum 70% cocoa solids), chopped
¾ tsp instant espresso powder
180ml double cream

To decorate
instant espresso powder
dark chocolate curls or shavings
chocolate-covered espresso beans (optional)

Grease the base of a deep 20cm springform cake tin and line with baking parchment.

For the base, melt the butter in a pan over a gentle heat. Crush the biscuits with a rolling pin or blitz in a food processor. Place the crumbs in a bowl, add the sugar, espresso powder and melted butter and stir to combine. Tip the base mixture into the prepared tin and level with the back of a metal spoon. Chill for 30 minutes.

Place the chocolate in a heatproof bowl over a pan of simmering water, making sure it doesn't touch the water. Melt the chocolate, stirring occasionally. Remove from the heat and allow to cool.

Using an electric hand-held mixer, beat together the cream cheese, icing sugar and vanilla extract in a large bowl until smooth. Sift in the cocoa powder and beat until combined. Fold in a spoonful of the cooled chocolate until combined then fold in the rest of the chocolate. Gradually pour in the cream, whisking continuously, until thick and smooth. Scrape down the sides of the bowl to ensure all of the cream cheese is mixed together. Spoon the mixture over the biscuit base, smoothing it out with a spatula or the back of a spoon. Chill in the fridge for at least 4 hours, until set.

When set, make the ganache topping. Put the chocolate and espresso powder into a bowl and set aside. Place the cream in a small saucepan over a low-medium heat and bring to a low simmer – don't let it boil. Pour the cream over the chocolate and leave it to melt for a minute. Slowly whisk the cream through, moving in the same direction, until combined and smooth. Set aside to cool for 6–8 minutes before pouring onto the cheesecake. Gently tilt the cheesecake tin to enable the ganache to spread across the top. Chill in the fridge for 30–40 minutes until set.

Partly unclip the tin and gently slide a small palette knife around the edge of the cake to loosen. Fully open the tin and remove the cake. You may need to smooth the edges with the palette knife. Decorate the top of the cake with a little espresso powder, chocolate curls or shavings and chocolate-covered espresso beans (if using).

Barbecued Peach Melba

Originally invented by a French chef at the Savoy, peach Melba has always been a British favourite, and I loved it as a child. This is my version for the barbecue – it's easy to prepare and the perfect dessert to cook as the flames die back on the barbecue. The hot, sticky peaches with the texture of the nuts and the sweet tart raspberry sauce is a real delight, and the black pepper adds a surprising burst of aromatic spice. If it's not a day for a barbecue, the peach parcels can be baked in the oven at 200°C/180°C fan/gas 6 for 12–15 minutes.

SERVES 4

300g fresh raspberries, plus extra to serve
1–2 tbsp icing sugar
zest and juice of ½ lemon
4 ripe peaches, halved and stoned
a small knob of butter
2 tbsp brown sugar
runny honey, for drizzling
freshly cracked black pepper
4–8 scoops of vanilla ice cream
3 tbsp flaked almonds, toasted

Put the raspberries in a food processor or blender and blitz until well puréed. Strain through a sieve into a bowl, pressing down on the solids to release the juice. Sift 1 tablespoon of icing sugar into the purée and whisk until fully combined. Stir through a squeeze of lemon juice to taste and adjust for sweetness if needed. (If you have any raspberry gin, Chambord or Framboise liqueur, feel free to add a splash!) Chill until ready to serve.

Prepare four squares of heavy-duty kitchen foil and place two halves of peach on each, cut-side up. Dot each with a little butter, spoon ¼ tablespoon of brown sugar over each peach half, sprinkle over the lemon zest and finish each with a drizzle of honey and a pinch of cracked pepper. Gather up the sides of the foil to create a parcel and scrunch to seal the packets.

Place the peach parcels on the barbecue grill away from direct heat, or place in the dying embers, and cook for 10–15 minutes depending on the heat of your barbecue.

Arrange the peaches in four serving bowls, pouring over any cooking juices (or eat straight from the foil!). Top with a scoop or two of ice cream, drizzle with the raspberry sauce and scatter with the toasted almonds and extra fresh raspberries.

Caribbean Cinnamon Banana Fritters with Chocolate Sauce Dip

Childhood memories of my mum's kitchen come flooding back when I make these fritters. She used to make these banana treats with us kids hanging around in the kitchen, happily licking the cinnamon sugar from our fingers, waiting until the next batch was ready to eat! I've used a combination of plain and wholemeal flour in these vegan-friendly fritters, because I like the nuttiness, but use just plain if you prefer. I love serving them with my quick and easy chocolate sauce – it's like a Caribbean version of churros!

MAKES 14–16 FRITTERS

4 large, very ripe bananas
100g plain flour
50g wholemeal flour
2 tsp baking powder
1 heaped tbsp
    desiccated coconut
3 tbsp brown sugar
¼ tsp salt
½ tsp ground nutmeg
½ tsp ground cinnamon
½ tsp vanilla extract
oil, for deep-frying

For the chocolate sauce
75g dark chocolate, chopped
10g butter or plant-based
    butter
125ml double cream
    or plant-based cream
a pinch of ground cinnamon
½ tbsp golden syrup

To coat
4 tbsp caster sugar
2 tsp ground cinnamon

Put the bananas in a food processor and blitz to a smooth purée (or mash well with a fork). Scoop out into a bowl. Add the flours, baking powder and coconut and stir in the sugar and salt. Mix well until you have a creamy, thick batter, adding a little warm water if needed. Stir in the nutmeg, cinnamon and vanilla. Cover and allow to rest for 15 minutes.

Meanwhile make the chocolate sauce. Place all the ingredients in a small saucepan over a low-medium heat, stirring constantly until everything has melted together and formed a smooth, silky sauce. Remove from the heat.

Mix the caster sugar and cinnamon together in a shallow bowl.

Heat enough oil for deep-frying in a deep-fryer or deep, heavy-based saucepan, making sure it comes no more than two-thirds of the way up the saucepan, to 160°C. If you don't have a thermometer, check the temperature by dropping in a little batter – it should immediately sizzle and bubble gently.

Use a tablespoon to drop spoonfuls of the batter into the oil and fry in batches of 4 or 5 (don't overcrowd the pan). Cook for 1–2 minutes then turn over and cook for another 1–2 minutes or until golden brown. If they brown too quickly, reduce the heat. Remove with a slotted spoon and drain on kitchen paper while you cook the rest. Roll each fritter in the sugar and cinnamon mixture until lightly covered and serve warm with the chocolate sauce for dipping or drizzling.

Calypso Pineapple Upside-Down Cake with Coconut Custard

A twist on the classic upside-down pineapple cake, this is an easy cake full of tropical flavour for a real feel-good sensation. I've added a little hint of spiced rum that is most often infused with vanilla, cinnamon and nutmeg, which works perfectly with the sweet pineapple. The cake is wonderful on its own as an afternoon treat, but when served with my coconut milk custard it's a deliciously satisfying and comforting pudding.

SERVES 6

For the pineapple topping
50g butter, softened
50g soft brown sugar
1 tbsp spiced rum
(or dark if you prefer)
zest of ½ lime, plus
extra to decorate
4–6 pineapple rings
in juice, drained
and juice reserved
4–6 glacé or maraschino
cherries

For the cake
100g butter, softened
100g golden caster sugar
2 large eggs
100g self-raising flour
1 tsp baking powder
zest of ½ lime
a pinch of salt
1 tsp vanilla extract
2 tbsp spiced rum
(or dark if you prefer)

For the coconut custard
1 x 400ml tin coconut milk
1 egg
1 egg yolk
1½ tsp cornflour
50g caster sugar
½ tsp vanilla extract

Preheat the oven to 180°C/160°C fan/gas 4.

First, prepare your pineapple topping. In a bowl, beat together the butter and sugar, using an electric hand-held whisk, until smooth and creamy. Beat in the rum and lime zest. Spread evenly over the bottom and 1–2cm up the sides of a 20cm round fixed-base cake tin. Pat the pineapple rings dry and arrange on top of the buttered base. You may need to cut the slices in half to fit your tin. Put the cherries in the centre of each ring (you can add more to fill any gaps around the sides if you like).

Put the butter and sugar for the cake in a bowl and beat together until pale and soft. Add the eggs and beat well. Sift over the flour and baking powder, stir in the lime zest, salt, vanilla and rum and mix into a soft, smooth batter. Stir in 1 tablespoon of the reserved pineapple juice.

Spoon the cake mixture carefully into the tin on top of the pineapple and smooth it out gently so that it is level. Bake for 30–35 minutes until cooked through and golden.

Meanwhile, make the coconut custard. Put the coconut milk into a small pan over a low-medium heat and bring to a low simmer (don't let it boil). Whisk the egg, yolk, cornflour and sugar in a bowl then gradually whisk in the warm coconut milk. Pour the liquid through a sieve back into the pan, stir in the vanilla and return to a low-medium heat. Cook, stirring constantly, until thickened, then remove from the heat.

Remove the cake from the oven and transfer the tin to a wire rack to cool for 5 minutes. Gently ease a thin spatula or knife around the edge of the tin to loosen, put a large plate on top of the tin then carefully turn it over so the cake is the right way up… or upside down! Enjoy warm, sprinkled with a little more lime zest and served with the custard.

SIMPLE SIDES

Sun-Blushed Tomatoes

SERVES 4–6

250g baby plum or cherry
    tomatoes, halved
2 tsp picked thyme
    or oregano leaves
pinch of sugar
good-quality olive oil,
    for drizzling
sea salt

Preheat the oven to 140°C/120°C fan/gas 1. Line a baking tray with baking parchment.

Arrange the tomato halves cut-side up on the baking tray. Season with salt and sprinkle on the sugar. Scatter over the thyme or oregano leaves and drizzle over 1–2 tablespoons of olive oil. Roast in the oven for 2–2½ hours, depending on size, or until semi-dried.

Chickpea Salad

SERVES 4

3 tbsp olive oil
¼ tsp Kashmiri chilli powder
1 small garlic clove, minced
2 tsp runny honey
    or maple syrup
zest and juice of ½ lemon
1 x 400g tin chickpeas,
    drained and rinsed
2 vine tomatoes, de-seeded
    and chopped
½ cucumber, chopped
4–6 radishes, trimmed
    and chopped
2 spring onions,
    trimmed and sliced
a large handful of coriander,
    roughly chopped
10 mint leaves,
    roughly chopped
sea salt

In a small bowl, mix together the olive oil, chilli powder, garlic, honey, lemon zest and juice, and season with salt.

In a separate bowl, mix together the chickpeas and remaining salad ingredients.

When ready to serve, pour over the dressing and toss to coat. Check for seasoning.

Creamy Mash

SERVES 4–6

1.5kg Yukon Gold or
  Desiree Potatoes,
  peeled and chopped
  into chunks
75g butter
2 garlic cloves,
  minced (optional)
100ml milk
sea salt and freshly
  ground white pepper

Bring a large saucepan of salted water to the boil over a medium heat. Add the potatoes and cook for 14–16 minutes or until tender.

Meanwhile, in a small saucepan over a medium heat, melt the butter, add the garlic (if using) and cook for 30 seconds. Add the milk and bring to a gentle simmer.

Drain the potatoes well and leave in the colander to steam dry for a couple of minutes. Pass through a potato ricer back into the saucepan (or mash well with a potato masher). Pour the warm butter and milk mixture over the mashed potatoes and beat well with a wooden spoon until you have a smooth, creamy mash. Season to taste with salt and white pepper.

Sweet Potato Wedges

SERVES 4

3–4 large sweet potatoes,
  scrubbed and cut
  lengthways into wedges
olive oil, for drizzling
flaky sea salt
cayenne pepper or sweet
  smoked paprika

Preheat the oven to 200°C/180°C fan/gas 6.

Place the sweet potato wedges in a bowl, drizzle with olive oil and season with salt. Toss to coat, then arrange on a baking tray in a single layer. Bake for 25–30 minutes, turning once, until golden and crispy. Sprinkle with cayenne pepper or paprika and a little more salt to serve.

Chilli & Garlic Cavolo Nero

SERVES 4

600g cavolo nero (or Savoy
cabbage or chard), tough
stems removed, roughly
shredded
3 tbsp extra-virgin olive oil
2 garlic cloves, thinly sliced
1 small red chilli, de-seeded
and thinly sliced
zest and juice of ½ lemon
sea salt and freshly ground
black pepper

Bring a large pan of salted water to the boil over a medium-high heat. Add the cavolo nero and blanch for 1–2 minutes, then drain and plunge into cold water to refresh. Drain and pat dry.

Add the oil to a large, deep frying pan over a medium-high heat. Add the garlic and chilli and fry for 1 minute, then add the lemon zest and juice, then the cavolo nero, tossing to coat. Season and cook for 3–4 minutes, stirring and adding a splash of water if needed. The cabbage should be wilted and coated in the oil.

Vichy-Style Carrots

SERVES 4–6

750g carrots, peeled and
cut on the diagonal
into 2cm slices
pared zest of 1 lemon
(using a swivel peeler)
1 thyme sprig
40g butter
2 tsp caster sugar
2 tbsp chopped
flat-leaf parsley
sea salt and freshly
ground black pepper

Put the carrots, strips of lemon zest, thyme, butter and sugar in a small, heavy-based saucepan. Pour over just enough water to cover, cover with a lid and bring to a fast boil over a medium-high heat. Reduce the heat and simmer, uncovered, for 12–14 minutes or until the carrots are tender and the liquid has evaporated to a small amount of glaze over the carrots, tossing the carrots to coat as it reduces (if the carrots aren't quite tender, add a splash of water to continue cooking). Remove the lemon zest, season to taste and sprinkle over the parsley to serve.

Peas & Onions

SERVES 4

50g butter
1 onion, finely chopped
500g frozen petits pois
or garden peas
5 tbsp chicken or
vegetable stock
a pinch of sugar
sea salt and freshly
ground black pepper

Melt half the butter in a deep-sided frying pan or sauté pan over a medium heat, add the onion and cook for 4–6 minutes until softened but not coloured. Tip in the peas and add the stock and sugar. Season to taste and simmer gently for 3–4 minutes until the peas are tender and the liquid has evaporated. Stir in the remaining butter, check the seasoning and serve.

ACKNOWLEDGEMENTS

How wonderful it was to get back together with the team to work on another exciting series – so big thanks to Leanne Clarke and all at ITV. It was great to get out and about around the UK to film with some of the country's most passionate food producers. Thanks to them all for taking part and a big thumbs up to chef Joseph Denison Carey too. We were also very lucky to film at the Carbis Bay Hotel in Cornwall with its beautiful beach location and great hospitality.

A special thank you to our fabulous executive producer David Nottage, Charlotte Davis and the entire team at Rock Oyster Media – from the people in the production office (shoutout to Fran, Olwyn and Meg) to all the team on location – you are the best! Series producer and absolute star Hannah Wilson, director Matt Wheeler and the crew – Rob, Jonny, James, Matt P and the shed – thank you all for making everything run so smoothly, cheers for the laughs and always keeping up the good mood! Big love and thanks to my fantastically well-organised home economist, Claire Bassano, and her kitchen dream team, Lola and Yasmin.

To my publisher Laura Higginson, editor Lisa Pendreigh and all involved at Penguin Random House and Ebury Press, thank you for your hard work and making this book happen under the very tightest of deadlines. We did it!

To Dan Jones, for his beautiful food photography and for making me look pretty damn good on the cover! To food stylist Bianca Nice, props stylist Max Robinson, designers Alex and Emma at Smith & Gilmour, for making everything look so gorgeous and yummy.

To my wonderful family and friends – thank you for your love and patience and for being the most excellent food tasters. My dog, Bobby, for being a very good boy and, as always, a very special thank you to my family at JHA – Jerry, Sarah, Julie and, of course, Charlotte – I couldn't have done it without your inspiration and support.

Last, but by no means least, a huge thanks to you guys at home for watching and cooking Ainsley's Good Mood Food!

Love and hugs, Ainsley xxx